Denver Delicious
by Katie Stapleton

Illustrations by Judy M. Disner

JOHNSON BOOKS: BOULDER

ISBN 0-933472-59-5

Typesetting and graphics by Typographics West, Inc.

Printed in the United States of America by
Johnson Publishing Company
1880 South 57th Court
Boulder, Colorado 80301

DEDICATION

with love, appreciation and admiration

To Mother, who does not know how to boil water, but who has taught me how to face all the challenges of life, including boiling water.

Contents

PART I
OLD DENVER CUISINE
CHAPTER I
Homage to Molly Brown
Denver's Hostess with the Mostess
(1867-1932)

CHAPTER II
Homage to Clara Mitchell
Denver's Reigning Hostess
(1865-1944)

i

CHAPTER III
Other Old-Time Recipes from Denver's Bygone Days

PART II
COOKING FOR TODAY
CULINARY DENVER IN TRANSITION

CHAPTER IV
Picnics and Backyard Frolics
(Alias Barbecues)

CHAPTER V
Crêpes

CHAPTER VI
Mile-High Soufflés

CHAPTER VII
The Egg, Etcetera

CHAPTER VIII
Denver Dividends

CHAPTER IX
The Coffee Bag

CHAPTER X
Denver Hospitable

Preface

Perhaps even more than in bygone days, the very name, Denver, electrifies many of us. As a Denver transplant and convert, married to a Denver native, I have always been very proud of our city and greatly contented with the community where we have always lived, worked and brought up our children.

Concomitant with Denver's growth is, of course, a renewed interest in living well. Not only is living well life's best revenge, but it is also the best way to preserve civilization for civilized human beings. We cooks everywhere should daily reaffirm our reverence for the Good Earth— God's creation—as we use its resources prudently in the service of others. This means, of course, that the ideal must be to do the very best we can with nature's bounty to preserve and present it in all its full seasonal glory.

We all realize that delicious food and drink not only sustain life, but nurture the spirit as well. The pleasures of the table provide an important time for refreshment amid beauty, laughter, consideration and relaxation. Whether sharing food together at a family dinner or at a party, this rite of coming together to eat should be an integral part of daily living. For where and what you eat and how food is presented are fundamental to living well.

This cookbook is not meant to be an all-inclusive one and the recipes will not frighten away any cook. Contrived recipes are not for today's busy male and female cooks who may be juggling careers, running households and bringing up children, in addition to undertaking a multitude of personal and community chores and interests.

As you prepare these recipes, my ardent hope is that as you cook them, you will always try to do so with love. Remember that the preparation and serving of food demonstrates your love offered to your family and friends; and when you are offered food, please don't forget to compliment the cook to show your love and appreciation for all his or her trouble.

For cooks and diners alike, my wish is that you will find these recipes delicious and that you will enjoy each of them as much as I have enjoyed preparing, cooking and serving them at our house.

Katie

Part I

Old Denver Cuisine

Homage to Molly Brown

Chapter I

Denver's Hostess with the Mostess (1867-1932)

Titanic
Molly Brown
Denver's Hostess
with the Mostess

Denver's storybook Molly Brown was recognized as a national and international figure in her own time, as well as remaining a lasting legend. In the years after her death, *"The Unsinkable Molly Brown"* was glamorized by the Broadway musical of the same name which celebrated her fearless exploits. She was also honored by having her name emblazoned on the space capsule, Gemini III, which conquered uncharted territory, just as Molly did in her own time.

During her lifetime, Molly's fame and prestige grew considerably after she bravely survived the sinking of The Titanic. When this luxury liner had the misfortune to hit an iceberg, Molly helped others live through the ordeal of the rough seas in the small, perilous rowboats.

Her adoring husband, J.J. Brown—an early-day Colorado millionaire—made his fortune in mining. These funds provided Molly with the financial resources to maintain her incredible standard of high living. Besides her travels and stays in deluxe hotels abroad, Molly's costliest expenses were her lavish parties where she offered exclusively the most expensive food and wines served by her retinue of uniformed footmen, one stationed behind each guest's chair at the dining table.

Molly's family heritage of near poverty in her growing-up years at Hannibal, Missouri, followed by her escape to the mining camp at Leadville, Colorado, substantiates that she was not born with a silver spoon in her mouth. Although ridiculed socially and ostracized at first by Denver's elite (known as the *"Sacred 36"*) due to her humble background, she became an instant success with high society circles in both fashionable Newport and Paris. Molly was accepted because of her talent as a fabulous storyteller with a vivid imagination and her innate courage in never being intimidated by anyone, whether very wealthy, or belonging to top drawer society, or both.

Although unaccustomed to a fine table either in her formative years in Hannibal or in her early years at Leadville, Molly always scorned simple fare. Some connoisseurs of fine food are born so eager to enjoy the pleasures of the table that they have an inborn curiosity to learn how to prepare and serve food with style. So it was with Molly Brown.

Like all good cooks, Molly scribbled her recipes on scraps of papers which invariably were disorganized. Sadly, for history's sake, Molly's nephew-in-law burned most of her recipes at her death. Sad, too, for the sake of the store of original documents in the third most popular tourist attraction in Colorado – the restored Molly Brown House in Denver. Only a treasured few of Molly's recipes remain for us to emulate today.

The indomitable Molly did return home from her countless luxurious sojourns abroad, bringing new recipes to impress guests at her parties, as well as interjecting continental ideas of entertaining to Denver. She was solely responsible for bringing buffet service to Denver to serve large groups more easily. Buffet service was an immediate hit and a valuable legacy, not only to hosts and hostesses entertaining large groups at home, but also, buffet service is even now the backbone of Denver clubs and restaurants to facilitate service.

Sadly, the poignant aspect of Molly's parties was that, all too often, no one would come. She would be left with all her splendiferous food, wines and footmen amid empty chairs at table. Picture the scene of a hostess on the verge of, hopefully, a triumphant party, and how crushed she must have been at such cruel treatment. But after her heroic efforts to save others during the 1912 sinking of The Titanic, at long last, Denver's *"Sacred 36"* condescended to accept her. What an incredible feat it had been for Molly!

Since nostalgia is such a cherished feeling today, may I suggest this re-created menu of a Molly Brown Dinner Party for a party menu the next time it is your turn to host your gourmet club or when you want a special treat to entertain friends. Even fantasize that you are either Molly or J.J. Brown. If you don't want to go all the way serving this elaborate multi-course dinner, simply copy one of these recipes and sneak it into your next party menu.

What wine would Molly serve with a feast such as this? Like many experienced Denver hostesses today, Molly preferred to serve a different wine with each course with a special glass for each wine. But her passion was bubbly champagne. She thought that serving only champagne throughout the entire dinner was like Paradise. (I wouldn't deny it.) While you are dining sumptuously on food made from Molly's recipes, don't forget to toast dauntless Molly's culinary achievements.

Nostalgic Menu for
Molly Brown
Dinner Party

Oysters Imperial*
Blanc de Blancs 1976**

•

Molly Brown's Veal with Two Sauces
(from Hotel Bristol, Paris)

Wild Rice with Almonds

**Artichoke Soufflé Ring
with Sautéed Frenched Green Beans**

Cauliflower with Glazed Carrot Coins
Échezeaux 1969**

•

Light-as-a-Feather Icebox Rolls

•

Redbud Flower Salad

•

Baked Alaska Flambé
Dom Perignon Champagne**

•

Demitasse in the parlor for the ladies,
while the men remained at table to smoke cigars.

* Better substitute Broiled Oysters Vermouth (recipe follows the one for Oysters Imperial) unless you have just inherited a windfall and can withstand caviar's ridiculous price.

** Feel free to be patriotic and drink less costly California wines like three of my favorites: Stone Creek Chablis, Jordan Cabernet Sauvignon and Le Domaine Champagne.

Oysters Imperial

This recipe, discovered among Molly Brown's helter-skelter papers, was scrawled on the back of a faded 1910 Walter Damrosch concert program in Denver.

Today, as the availability of caviar shrinks and its price soars to several hundred dollars for a 12-oz. tin of Iranian Beluga Malossal Caviar, and since no bargains are to be discovered in American caviar either, you may well prefer to substitute another spiffy oyster dish such as Broiled Oysters Vermouth. But read on anyway and dream about how to create this recipe for Oysters Imperial. Then, make Broiled Oysters Vermouth.

4-6 oysters on their half shells
2-3 teaspoons black caviar
1-2 teaspoons fresh lemon juice
Pepper, freshly ground
1 teaspoon chives, minced

For One Serving
Cover each raw oyster on half shell with ½ teaspoon black caviar. Sprinkle with lemon juice, pepper and chives. Serve as a first course.

Broiled Oysters Vermouth

1 quart fresh small oysters
4 Tablespoons butter, melted
4 Tablespoons vermouth
4 Tablespoons lemon juice
Salt and pepper, freshly ground, to taste

GARNISH:
Parsley, minced

Serves 8
Preheat broiler.

Drain oysters and place in shallow pan over low heat. Drain off juice as it forms in the pan after only 1 to 2 minutes, after oysters have plumped. Remove pan from heat and marinate for 30 minutes in melted butter, vermouth, lemon juice, salt and pepper. Drain again, and reserve marinade.

Broil oysters about 5 minutes until edges curl and oysters are all well heated. Pour the heated vermouth marinade over oysters just before serving. Sprinkle with minced parsley for color and serve warm. Not too shabby a recipe after all.

Hint: Open oyster shells with a beer can opener—a miracle tool for the odious job. Or use a convection oven: heat oysters at 350° for 10 minutes.

Molly Brown's Veal with Two Sauces

Such a rich dish (can you imagine cooks today serving TWO sauces?) but utterly exquisite. Remember: in Molly Brown's time - in the world of food - more was far better than less.

8 veal chops
3 Tablespoons butter, softened

Serves 8

Preheat oven to 350°.

Place butter-coated chops in broiler pan. Bake in oven approximately 20 minutes. When veal is no longer pink and is fully cooked, remove veal chops to platter and keep warm. Reserve pan with juices for later use.

FOR THE MUSHROOM SAUCE:
1 onion, chunked
¼ lb. fresh mushrooms, cleaned
1 teaspoon tomato paste
Salt to taste
⅓ cup dry white wine
1 Tablespoon butter
2 Tablespoons flour

Meanwhile, into your food processor bowl fitted with steel blade, put onion chunks to process briefly. Add mushrooms. Process until puréed.

Put broiler pan where chops were cooked over low-medium heat on stove. Add mushroom-onion purée, tomato paste, salt and white wine. Add butter and whisk in flour to thicken. When sauce is smooth and thick, pour over chops and let stand to form a crust. Keep warm.

FOR THE CREAM SAUCE:
2 Tablespoons butter
2 Tablespoons flour
⅞ cup milk
1 egg, beaten
2 oz. Parmesan cheese, grated
Additional 2 Tablespoons
** butter, melted**
1 teaspoon paprika

In another pan on stove over medium heat, melt butter and whisk in flour to make roux. Gradually whisk in milk. Add more milk, if necessary, to make thick cream sauce. Take pan off stove. (This much may be done ahead, but cover top of sauce in pan with a round of wax paper to prevent a skin from forming. Remember to reheat veal chops.) Add beaten egg. Sauce must not boil after egg is added, but should be kept hot.

Return mushroom-sauced veal chops to original broiler pan. If necessary, place pan briefly in oven to reheat. Layer hot cream sauce over chops, but mushroom sauce and cream sauce should not mix. Sprinkle liberally with grated Parmesan cheese. Top with melted butter and paprika.

Wild Rice with Almonds

At the exorbitant price of wild rice today, it behooves every cook who indulges to learn how best to cook it. Strangely, even Minnesotans—where wild rice is most apt to be found in the marshes—cook it the wrong way.

The way to cook wild rice so that each kernel puffs and loses its bitiness is to follow this one single rule: *do not boil wild rice.* That's also when it gets mushy.

First, put wild rice in a bowl to wash it well with cold water until water is clear. Change the water when it becomes cloudy. Place wild rice in a heavy pan and pour boiling hot water over rice to cover. Cover pan tightly and do not peek. If you do, the steam will escape.

When the water cools, repeat process two or three more times until wild rice completely "butterflies" (each kernel opens). After that happens, cool rice and drain in a colander for several hours. Wild rice should be prepared a half day prior to using it in recipe. This opulent dish will please your most discerning guest, just as it pleased Molly's guests many years ago.

1 cup raw wild rice
   (makes about 3½ cups cooked
   wild rice)
1 small onion, chunked
2 Tablespoons chives
2 green peppers, top, membrane
   and seeds removed, coarsely
   cut
4 oz. butter
4 cups chicken stock, hot
Salt and pepper, freshly ground,
   to taste
½ cup blanched almonds,
   shredded

One 5-cup casserole

Serves 8

Prepare wild rice according to my directions, but for this recipe, pour boiling water over wild rice only two times.

Preheat oven to 300°.

Into your food processor bowl fitted with steel blade, and with motor running, drop onion, then chives and green peppers into feed tube. Process briefly until finely minced. Turn off motor as each ingredient is processed.

Sauté minced onion, chives and green peppers in melted butter. Add prepared wild rice. Add hot chicken stock, salt, pepper and almonds. Cook just long enough to heat.

Pour into casserole. Bake 1½ hours or until each kernel of wild rice is puffed up with chicken stock.

Artichoke Soufflé Ring

Served with sautéed Frenched green beans in the center of the unmolded ring mold, Artichoke Soufflé Ring becomes a marvelous contrast of textures: the crisp beans versus the smooth but thick soufflé texture - as was the custom in Molly's era - as well as a contrast of colors.

During Molly's visits to the Hotel Ritz, Paris's then most fashionable hotel, she wisely learned how ordinary vegetables could be glamorized as in this recipe.

**Three 8-oz. cans artichoke
  bottoms
3 Tablespoons butter
3 Tablespoons flour
1 cup cream, warmed
¾ teaspoon salt
6 egg yolks, lightly beaten
1½ cups fine cracker crumbs
6 egg whites**

**One 6½-cup ring mold
  buttered**

Serves 8

Preheat oven to 350°.

Place artichoke bottoms in sieve and wash quickly under cool running water to wash off preservatives. In food processor bowl fitted with steel blade, process artichoke bottoms until puréed.

Put butter in pan over low heat to melt and whisk in flour to make roux. Slowly add warm cream. (Cream should be warm to inside of your wrist.) Cook until sauce is thick.

Add salt and cook slightly. Stir in egg yolks; add cracker crumbs and fold in purée of artichoke bottoms.

Beat egg whites until stiff, not dry, and fold into artichoke mixture. Pour into ring mold and set in bain-marie (an outer pan filled with just-boiling water) in oven. Bake 45 minutes.

Unmold Artichoke Soufflé Ring on a circular platter for best effect.

Cauliflower with Glazed Carrot Coins

This waterless cooking technique in the carrot recipe is a neat way to cook vegetables to preserve their color, as well as to avoid overcooking them. For another study in contrast in color, as well as texture, a whole cauliflower or two adorned with carrot coins and surrounded with sprigs of parsley is unbeatable. Talk about Molly's glamorizing vegetables.

2 medium-size cauliflower heads
4-5 carrots
4 Tablespoons butter
3 Tablespoons honey or 6 Tablespoons sugar
Juice of half lemon

GARNISH:
Sprigs of fresh parsley

Serves 8

Discard stems of cauliflowers and any wilted outer leaves, but cook cauliflowers whole. Place in pan of already-boiling water and boil cauliflowers until just tender. Drain well.

You may also microwave cauliflowers. To accomplish this, put whole cauliflowers into a large glass pan, topped with tight plastic cover with ¼ cup water. Microwave about 12 minutes at simmer (50%). Turn dish once half-way through cooking. Cauliflowers will continue to cook with plastic cover left on 2 to 3 minutes after removing dish from microwave.

In food processor bowl fitted with slicer, stack peeled carrots vertically in feed tube until completely full. With mild pressure on pusher, process, making carrot rounds like coins.

To cook carrot coins, use waterless technique. Melt butter in a heavy bottomed pan. Add carrot coins, honey (or sugar) and lemon juice. Cover pan with a tight-fitting lid and cook over low heat to glaze carrots. If using honey, be careful lest honey boil.

As an alternative, carrots can be glazed in glass or microwave proof pan in microwave: first, melt butter in pan about 2 minutes at 100% power. Add carrots, honey or sugar and lemon juice to pan and microwave 10 minutes at simmer (50%). Carrots should be stirred once during cooking time. Remove dish from microwave but carrots will continue to cook 2 to 3 minutes.

Serve whole cauliflowers studded with carrot coins in vegetable dish or on platter, garnished with parsley sprigs.

Light-as-a-Feather Icebox Rolls

You know instantly this is an old-time recipe by the antiquated word "icebox"—the ancestor of all our hoity-toity refrigerators today. This recipe is still a star because of its practicality, not to overlook the fact that these rolls are light-as-a-feather.

⅔ cup shortening (not butter)
¾ cup sugar
1 cup boiling water
2 packages (2 Tablespoons) dry yeast*
1 cup very warm water
2 eggs, beaten
6-7 cups unbleached flour, sifted
½ teaspoon salt

***A note about yeast: One 1-oz. cake of fresh compressed yeast is equivalent to 2 packages (2 Tablespoons) of active dry yeast. Be sure to examine date on package of dry yeast before using. Cake yeast should be dissolved in lukewarm liquid but dry yeast requires very warm liquid.**

Makes 18 to 20 cloverleaf rolls

Cream together shortening and sugar in bowl of food processor fitted with steel blade. Add boiling water through feed tube and let mixture dissolve. Do not process again. Remove to another bowl. Cool.

Dissolve yeast in very warm water.

In food processor bowl, still fitted with steel blade, process mixture of beaten eggs, sifted flour and salt. Add shortening-sugar mixture and process to combine. With motor running, pour yeast through feed tube. Dough will be gummy. Be careful not to overprocess. Remove dough to large greased bowl and cover tightly with plastic wrap. Refrigerate at least overnight and not longer than one week.

About three hours before serving (time depends on day's humidity): Grease muffin tins. Take dough out of icebox and make into cloverleaf rolls. Take three small balls of dough, and put side by side to make one muffin. (As dough rises, cloverleaves will come together.) Cover with damp tea towel. Let dough rise.

Preheat oven to 425°.

Bake muffins about 15 minutes.

10

Redbud Flower Salad

This recipe is my addition to Molly Brown's Menu because it is so unusual, so exotic, so pretty, and so spring-time seasonal that Molly herself would have loved to serve it.

Redbud Flower Salad will pique the curiosity of your guests, not to mention their palates.

2 cups freshly picked redbud flowers from a redbud tree* (wash flowers gently if tree has been sprayed)
1 apple, thinly sliced, peel left on for color
¾ cup golden raisins, plumped 10 minutes in ½ cup dry white wine
1 large head Bibb lettuce, cored, torn into bite-size pieces
¾ cup homemade mayonnaise

*If redbud flowers are unavailable, substitute coarsely chopped pecans. Need I comment that the taste will be completely different?

Serves 8

In salad bowl, combine all ingredients except flowers and toss delicately. Divide and serve salad to each guest on a chilled glass salad plate. Top with sprinkling of redbud flowers.

Baked Alaska Flambé

Molly Brown saw this spectacular dessert in 1900 at an elegant party in honor of Belgian King Leopold at Hotel Majestic in Paris. Mr. and Mrs. Horace Bennett, the late famed owners of the renowned Wolhurst estate near Denver, were also guests at the same party. Many Baked Alaska Flambés were served and Mrs. Bennett remembered that all those brandy-filled eggshell cups blazing away looked like "fire burning on snow". Don't you wish you'd been there, too? But don't despair because you can now serve this glamorous dessert at your house.

PREPARE A DAY AHEAD:
NATURALIZED SPONGE CAKE
6 egg yolks
1 Tablespoon orange zest,
 grated
½ cup orange juice
½ cup honey, warmed (warm
 in glass measuring cup in
 microwave, 45 seconds at
 low - 20%)
1⅜ cups cake flour
¼ teaspoon salt
6 egg whites
1 teaspoon cream of tartar
Additional 2 Tablespoons
 honey, warmed (microwave
 20 seconds at 20%)

2 round 9″ cake pans,
 lightly greased and floured
One cookie sheet

Serves 8-10
Preheat oven to 400°.

In a bowl of an electric mixer, or with a hand-held electric beater, beat egg yolks at high speed about 5 minutes. Add orange zest, juice and honey and beat another 5 minutes. Beat until mixture is very thick and smooth—about 12 to 15 minutes. Do not underbeat, as the lightness of this sponge cake depends on this beating process.

Sift flour. To measure flour correctly, measure after dipping into sifted flour with ½ cup measure. Level ½ cup measure with knife. Repeat process once. Then measure ⅜ cup in ½ cup measure. (Have an imaginary line between ¼ and ½ cup.) Add salt. Stir flour mixture into egg yolk mixture. Reserve.

Beat egg whites until foamy. Add cream of tartar and beat until mixture forms soft peaks. Gradually add additional warmed honey and beat until mixture is stiff. Use rubber spatula to fold egg whites gently and thoroughly into egg yolk mixture.

Pour sponge cake mixture into prepared cake pans. Bake about 15 to 20 minutes or until top of cake is lightly browned and an inserted straw comes out clean. Watch cakes toward end of baking, as honey is apt to burn. If cakes become too brown, cover each with aluminum foil.

FOR THE ICE CREAM LAYER:
1½ qts. vanilla ice cream, softened

JUST BEFORE SERVING:
FOR THE MERINGUE:
**6 egg whites (reserve
  6 halved eggshell cups)
1 teaspoon cream of tartar
2 Tablespoons honey, warmed**

FOR A HOLLYWOOD
PRESENTATION:
½ cup (or more) brandy

When sponge cakes have cooled more than an hour, invert onto a cookie sheet. With a plastic spatula, spoon softened ice cream to cover tops and sides of both layers. Place one layer on top of the other. Store the cake on cookie sheet in deep freeze. After about 12 hours, inspect to see if cake needs more ice cream.

Preheat oven to 500°.
   Beat egg whites until peaked, and then add cream of tartar and honey. Continue beating until stiff, not dry.
   Remove cake from freezer. Using a metal cake spatula, frost cake with meringue and place in oven 5 to 7 minutes or less. Watch carefully so that cake will turn golden brown and not scorch.

   Place clean empty eggshell halves symmetrically on top of Baked Alaska. Heat brandy in small pan until just warm. Pour warmed brandy into each eggshell. Pour remaining heated brandy over cake and ignite. Ignite brandy in eggshells so your guests are treated to a full pyrotechnical display.

**Homage
to
Molly
Brown**

13

Homage
to
Clara
Mitchell

Denver's Reigning Hostess (1865-1944)

Chapter II

Why Clara Mitchell Was Vital to Denver

In the nineties, Denver was transformed from a frontier town into the social capital of a growing empire. Its upper crust lived in a rarefied atmosphere that was a mixture of the sophistication of the various capitals of the world, tinged with a unique western flavor.

As the mining kings and their wives moved into the Queen City from Leadville, Central City, and other bonanzas, their mansions became the centers of social activity, always presided over by the lady-of-the-house.

Exemplary of this golden era was Clara Goodell, originally from Leadville, who married John Clark Mitchell, a lifelong Colorado banker. Starting as a bank clerk, his genius in banking became apparent over the years. He eventually served as president of Denver National Bank (1913-1925), as well as being a director of the Federal Reserve Bank. He was very active in civic affairs.

Clara was one of the four Goodell sisters from Leadville who married young men, though obscure at the time, all were destined to become prominent in the building of the Rocky Mountain Empire. Probably the most vital and vivacious of all the Goodell sisters was Clara. As John Mitchell's wife, she entertained lavishly and was Denver's undisputed reigning hostess of her era. Her hospitality and selfless zeal were models, not only for her two children, but for all the other hostesses in the Queen City.

The four-story white brick colonial Mitchell mansion was considered one of the most beautiful on Quality Hill. This mansion with its playroom, dubbed Hilarity Hall, was the scene of incredible parties; certainly no one was known to ever refuse an invitation from Clara and John. A great number of guests, as well as three generations of Mitchells, enjoyed themselves to the hilt in Hilarity Hall. The room was a combination cardroom, playroom and ballroom—all in red and black.

Decorated in green and white,the inviting drawing room had recessed ceiling lights and a gigantic rare beaded-prism crystal chandelier which was the center of the room. Besides Hilarity Hall, the dining room was the most striking: the lower walls were paneled and the ceilings were beamed in white woodwork with brown. Above the high panels, the walls were covered with brocaded yellow velvet. The mahogany-walled library was lightened by a blue and gold fabric. But John Mitchell's favorite room was his small den, off one end of the long hall dividing the rooms.

John Mitchell died in 1925, and Clara continued to live in her mansion, attended by her maids and chauffeur, who once had been the family's coachman. Their devotion to Clara in her later years was another recognition of Clara's warm and generous personality.

During World War II, Clara Mitchell's home became the center for Red Cross work when Hilarity Hall was converted into a nursing school. Clara thus showed her flexibility ranging from Denver's reigning hostess to a model civic volunteer in wartime.

Her daughter, Clara Mitchell Van Schaack Humphreys has continued many of her mother's fine traditions as Denver's most prominent hostess and civic worker in the half-century between 1930-1980. Recalling her mother, she says "My mother had a genius for homemaking and her foods were the highlight of our social functions. To raise money for one of her pet charities, Y.W.C.A., she published a cookbook, *The Way to a Man's Heart*, and tested every recipe in her own kitchen."

Clara's cookbook, *The Way to a Man's Heart*, was very successful and was frequently used in many Colorado kitchens, not only for her recipes, but because of what she typified for Coloradoans.

Here is a sampling of her menus combined with her appropriate shopping lists, all taken word-for-word from her cookbook, *The Way to a Man's Heart*. Thus, you may pretend to savor the extraordinary varied food she served and notice the copious amounts. These samplings are verbatim including Clara's original punctuation.

**Homage
to
Clara
Mitchell**

Quoted from *The Way to a Man's Heart*

Clara Mitchell's Buffet Luncheon for 75

16 quarts bouillon

For salad

15 pounds chicken,
12 large stalks celery or 3 dozen small ones,
2 quart bottles olive oil,
18 eggs, yolks,
Mayonnaise dressing.

1 turkey, 13 pounds,
2 cans mushrooms,
180 New York Counts, (oysters)
6½ dozen patty cases,
2 quarts cream sauce
2 pounds fancy cakes,
1 large cake,
2 pounds almonds,
1 small cake,
6 quarts sherbet (fruit),
7 quarts ice cream,
2 quarts plain cream,
1 pound tea,
3 quarts milk,
½ pound cocoa,
1½ pounds mints,
6 lemons.

Chafing Dish Supper for 40 People

8 quarts bouillon,
6 dozen frogs' legs,   1 quart cream,
7 mallard ducks for salmi of duck,   1 pint sherry wine,
20 stoned olives,
1 tablespoonful extract of beef for coloring,
150 New York Counts for frying,
16 pounds of turkey or 1 baked ham,
120 biscuits or rolls,   3 pounds butter,
2 pounds coffee,
3 pounds loaf sugar,   2 quarts coffee cream,
1½ pounds salted almonds,   1 bottle olives or pickles

Here are some special recipes from Clara Mitchell's book that I have adapted for easier preparation.

Macaroni Honeycomb Timbale

Creating this beehive requires infinite concentration and patience, not to forget the cook's time, but the finished product is both novel and spectacular for your buffet table.

Clara Mitchell's daughter, Clara Humphreys - Denver's Grand Dame after 1950 - continually used this recipe for her grand scale of entertaining. Like mother, like daughter.

10-oz. package of Mostaccioli macaroni
1½ teaspoons salt
1 Tablespoon oil
8 oz. butter, at room temperature

One 3-pt. ovenproof mold, conical shape to simulate beehive

Serves 10-12

Cook macaroni in large pan of boiling water to which salt and oil have been added. Cook to al dente stage (bitey)—firm and chewy. Drain macaroni in colander under cold running water to wash off starch.

Preheat oven to 325°.

With scissors, cut pieces of slantwise Mostaccioli to ¾ inch long each. Cut the sides straight.

Butter heavily (¼ to ½ inch thick) the bottom and sides of the mold. Line inside bottom of mold with upright cooked macaroni pieces: beginning in the center, insert upright macaroni pieces in butter in circular fashion. Continue in concentric circles until the bottom and the sides of the mold are filled. (Clara Van Schaack Humphreys uses toothpicks to apply her macaroni pieces to the buttered mold.)

The inside of the mold is now magically transformed into a honeycomb. Put mold into freezer to chill completely (at least 4 hours).

When filling is prepared, take mold out of freezer and fill with Celeriac Timbale. Bake in bain-marie 20 to 30 minutes.

When baked, invert monochrome mold onto platter and behold! A honeycomb. Surround with watercress or parsley or fresh green peas for color contrast.

This dish is extremely tricky to make, but don't despair if it isn't perfect, because you can patch up your honeycomb if it breaks off in spots. Try not to let the butter in which macaroni pieces are implanted melt during baking and run. If this should occur, rush mold into your freezer briefly. But no swearing, please, if you do not achieve your majestic honeycomb first time around. Keep at it and you'll succeed.

19

Celeriac Timbale Filling

This is my suggestion for the filling for Macaroni Honeycomb Timbale. Actually, it has such a compelling and different taste that served alone, it makes an epicurean accompaniment to meat, poultry or fish.

**2-3 celeriac (celery roots),
   peeled**
½ teaspoon fresh lemon juice
3 Tablespoons milk
2 slices bread, crusts removed
**2 Tablespoons butter,
   melted**
2 teaspoons onion, grated
4 egg yolks, beaten
Salt to taste
Dash of paprika
**⅛ teaspoon nutmeg,
   freshly grated**
4 egg whites

Cut up peeled celeriac and place in large pan of already-boiling water to cook for about 10 minutes. After celeriac is cooked and drained, sprinkle lemon juice over celery root to preserve color.

Pour milk into pan or saucer and soak bread in milk.

With a food processor bowl fitted with shredder, fill feed tube with cooked celeriac and process with medium pressure on pusher. Remove celeriac to another bowl. Combine with soaked, cut up bread, melted butter, grated onion, beaten egg yolks, salt, paprika and nutmeg.

Whip egg whites until stiff, not dry. Fold them carefully into celeriac mixture. Pour into Honeycomb Macaroni-filled mold and bake 20 to 30 minutes in bain-marie, 325° oven.

Variation: A fish, chicken or meat timbale also would be well worth trying as a filling.

Mitchell Crabmeat Canapés

This ageless recipe from Clara Mitchell's cookbook written 75 years ago is still sensational. Clara and her peers thought, in the Molly Brown tradition, that in the world of food, more was always preferable to less.

Serve a pair of these rounds or canapés as an enticing opening course or, if you prefer to pass them as hors d'oeuvre during the cocktail hour, increase the recipe by one and a half (150%) since they are very popular.

8 slices white bread,
 thinly sliced, crusts removed
1 Tablespoon butter
2 Tablespoons sardine paste,
 from one 1½-oz. can
 (If unavailable, make from
 sardines in olive oil. Use
 steel blade of food processor.)
1 teaspoon fresh lemon juice
3-4 plum tomatoes or
 5-6 cherry tomatoes
4 oz. crabmeat
2 Tablespoons mayonnaise
⅛ teaspoon salt
½ teaspoon paprika

Serves 8 as first course

Toast slices of bread on one side under broiler. Cut each slice into two rounds with plain round 2-inch cutter. Butter toasted rounds while hot. Spread each round with sardine paste. Sprinkle with lemon juice.

Top each prepared round with thin slice of ripe tomato. Do not add tomato slices until just before serving, lest toast become soggy.

Mix crabmeat and mayonnaise. Add salt and heap mixture on top of tomato slice on each round. Sprinkle paprika lightly on top.

**Homage
to
Clara
Mitchell**

Sunlight Strawberry Preserves

A great energy saver—light years ahead of its time as a recipe.

Do not double or triple this recipe, according to Clara Mitchell: just make it again and again.

2 cups sugar or
  1½ cups honey
½ cup water
2 cups choice strawberries,
  washed, then hulled

Jelly jars

Makes about 1½ pints

If using sugar, make syrup by combining sugar with water. Boil 2 minutes, then add strawberries. Boil mixture 5 to 7 minutes. Pour out on a platter (spread no thicker than 2 inches) and place outdoors in the sun daily. Cover with a screen to inhibit insects. Return platter indoors at night. Liquid will slowly evaporate and berries will be infused and swollen with heavy syrup. This process will take 3 to 4 days.

If using honey, put strawberries alone in boiling water. Boil 5 to 7 minutes. Remove pan, add honey and stir until honey is dissolved. The flavor and texture will be better when honey does not boil. Then, follow the same process as with sugar: pour mixture on platter and let stand daily in sun until syrup resembles a soft jelly. Pour into ½ pint sterilized jars, and seal tightly.

Also in her book, right on the heels of these gourmand menus and recipes, is included a section on "Useful Remedies". Actually, this inclusion is a typical sign of cookbooks of her era. For a glimpse of her remedies and how her other household prescriptions were concocted, here is another verbatim glimpse into *The Way to a Man's Heart:*

Hair Tonic

½ pint rosemary,
4 oz. cologne or bay rum,
1 oz. tincture of cantharides,
  (also known as Spanish fly),
1 oz. menthol,

Apply after shampoo.

For Mosquito Bites

⅓ alcohol,
⅓ ammonia,
⅓ camphor,

Mix all together.

Liniment for Lameness in Arms

10¢ worth best lard,
10¢ worth turpentine,
10¢ worth ammonia.

Melt lard and mix together; rub on lame part.

Other remedies are for Hemorrhoids, a Nerve Remedy, Cough Cure, Furniture Polish, Mothpowder and Sties. Quite a gamut and all these "Useful Remedies" follow Clara's recipes for her rich dishes included in her cookbook.

Remember the menus and useful remedies are quoted word-for-word from Clara Mitchell. Her successful book went into many succeeding printings.

Clara Mitchell represented the epitome of culinary leadership and talented hosting and was the model of top drawer society and civic leadership to which Denverites of her time aspired.

Other Old-Time Recipes from Denver's Bygone Days

Chapter III

Observations on Harvesting Old-Time Recipes

These recipes - scrupulously harvested from notable Denver hostesses - span a time frame from the turn of the nineteenth century through the first half of the twentieth.

After reading and devouring ideas from scads of old family cookbooks and old recipes on cards and bits of paper, generously loaned to me by families and descendants, two impressions stand paramount:

My first comment is that our forebearers had no clue as to what consuming so much rich food did to the body's cholesterol and triglycerides. Even though I have already downgraded the ingredients in these recipes with a watchful eye to nutrition, you may wish to adjust them even further, because they are exercises in excess.

Secondly, a conclusion from this research: neither our generation nor our children's has a corner on super entertaining and fine food. In truth, culinarily speaking, there is nothing new under the sun.

These Denver hostesses whose recipes are included did not actually cook these dishes themselves. In fact, almost none did! But each hostess definitely had a special knack with food and supervised very carefully everyone who cooked in her kitchen. In those days, the kitchen was completely the domain of the lady of the house.

As you choose any of these recipes to prepare for your family and friends, give a tip of your whisk in appreciation to these fine Western cooks, who have preceded us, for their culinary inspiration.

Scotch Woodcock

This authentic English dish – brought to the west in the early days – will make a delectable light supper or an engaging first course.

8 slices bread, toasted
  on one side, crusts removed
4 Tablespoons anchovy paste
3 Tablespoons butter
6 egg yolks
1 cup cream
¼ teaspoon salt
¼ teaspoon pepper

GARNISH:

Parsley, chopped

Serves 8

Spread each toasted side of bread with anchovy paste. Cut toast into three fingers.

Melt butter in top of double boiler. Beat together egg yolks with cream, salt and pepper. Add egg yolk mixture to melted butter and scramble until just creamy.

Arrange three fingers of anchovy toast on small individual heated plates and cover with egg mixture. Garnish with chopped parsley. Serve hot.

Glazed Canadian Bacon

Glazed Canadian Bacon is a perennial treat for a luxurious breakfast or brunch.

This recipe for Glazed Canadian Bacon, along with a few others in this chapter, is a cherished legacy from a fabulous Denver hostess and cook, my revered cousin, Berenice Mackenzie.

2-3 lb. slab Canadian
  bacon
½ cup beer and additional
  beer to make paste
¾ cup brown sugar
  or ½ cup honey
½ teaspoon dry mustard

Serves 8

Preheat oven to 350°.

Place Canadian bacon, fat side up, in a small heat-proof pan. Pour over it ½ cup beer and bake for 45 minutes. Baste meat occasionally with beer in pan.

Combine sugar or honey, dry mustard and enough beer to make a smooth paste. Remove Canadian Bacon from oven. Spread glaze over it. Return to oven an additional 20 minutes and continue to baste.

27

How to Dress Up a Ham

One of the primary reasons ham has sometimes been scorned over the years is that all too often it is poorly cooked. Going to all the trouble of making this recipe for Dressed Up Ham will produce a moist, succulent ham that will be long remembered by your guests.

**PREPARE HAM NIGHT
  BEFORE BAKING:**
One 10-lb. uncooked ham
12-oz. dark molasses
½ gallon weak tea
1 teaspoon ground cloves

**THE DAY HAM WILL
  BE SERVED:**
4 cups water

FOR THE COATING:
1 cup tomato catsup
3 Tablespoons Dijon mustard
One bottle beer or ale
3 Tablespoons brown sugar

**Serves 25 (One lb. of ham
  usually serves 2-3)**
Pour molasses over ham in roaster. Pour on weak tea in which ground cloves have been soaked. Let ham marinate at least 12 hours.

Preheat oven to 325°.
Remove ham from marinade and put in clean roaster, skin side down. Pour in water. Cover roaster tightly and bake 2 hours.

Set oven at 300°.
Take ham from roaster; pour off excess liquid and remove skin from ham. Spread ham with mixture of catsup and mustard. Return ham to roaster and bake at least an additional 30 minutes. Baste with beer every 10 minutes. Pour off beer at end of 30 minutes. Pat brown sugar into fat side of ham and return to oven until thoroughly cooked. (A 10-lb. uncooked ham should bake 3 to 3½ hours and meat thermometer should register 160°.) Remove ham from oven and place on carving platter. Remember to let ham rest about 20 minutes after baking, so it will be easier to carve.

For The Piccalilli Sauce:

Piccalilli Sauce is a must to pour over Dressed Up Ham or to use as an excellent embellishment for duck or game. Don't forget to serve this different old-fashioned sauce often.

One 9-oz. jar piccalilli
One 10-oz. jar currant
  jelly
1 Tablespoon dry mustard

Yield: about 2¼ cups
Stir ingredients together and heat until warm. Serve warm.

Baked Ham à la Kirkpatrick

This favored recipe, from a prominent Virginia navy hostess, accompanied her to Denver after World War II, when she and her Navy Captain husband chose Denver as their permanent home. No wonder she treasured the recipe, as it is a quickie, producing sensational results with ham.

**One 10-lb. baked ham,
  slightly underdone**
1 lb. brown sugar
1 teaspoon ground cloves
1 orange, sliced
1 lemon, sliced
**One 14-oz. bottle of
  catsup**

Serves 25
Preheat oven to 300°.
Remove skin from ham and pat ham with mixture of brown sugar and ground cloves. With a toothpick, affix slices of orange and lemon to the fat of the ham to add flavor. Cover ham with entire bottle of catsup. Bake 30 to 40 minutes. Remove ham from oven and place on carving platter. Remember to let ham rest about 20 minutes after baking, so it will be easier to carve.

Other
Old-Time
Recipes
from
Denver's
Bygone
Days

Shrimp and Rice

When you serve this old-fashioned western recipe, top with chutney. That makes the whole dish glow.

2 Tablespoons butter
2 cups cooked rice
**1 cup heavy cream
  (could substitute half-
  and-half)**
4 Tablespoons tomato catsup
2 Tablespoons chili sauce
**2 Tablespoons Worcestershire
  sauce**
$\frac{1}{8}$ teaspoon Tabasco
**Salt and pepper, freshly
  ground, to taste**
**2 cups fresh shrimp, cleaned,
  cut into bite-size pieces**
**2 Tablespoons onion, chopped,
  sautéed in butter**
**2 Tablespoons bread crumbs
  (use metal blade in food
  processor)**
3-4 Tablespoons chutney

One 6-cup casserole, oiled

Serves 8
Preheat oven to 350°.
Melt butter in top of double boiler. Stir in rice; add cream. When very hot, add catsup, chili sauce, Worcestershire sauce, Tabasco, salt and pepper. Let mixture cook a few minutes. Add shrimp and sautéed onion.
Pour shrimp mixture into casserole and cover with bread crumbs. Bake in oven 30 to 40 minutes.

Artichoke Hearts Gratinés

Artichoke Hearts Gratinés continue to make an impressive vegetable dish. Your family and guests will rave! Enjoy!

**2 packages frozen
    artichoke hearts or
    3 cans (14-oz.)
    artichoke hearts packed
    in brine, not oil
3 Tablespoons butter, cut up
3 Tablspoons flour
2 cups milk
⅛ teaspoon dry mustard
1 teaspoon onion juice***
**Salt and white pepper, to
    taste
1 egg, beaten
½ cup Swiss cheese, grated
2 Tablespoons bread crumbs
¼ teaspoon paprika**

***Onion juice is obtained by heavily salting the cut end of onion and then scraping onion with a knife as juice is released.**

Serves 6 to 8

Preheat oven to 350°.

If using frozen artichoke hearts, defrost and cook artichoke hearts according to package directions until barely done. If using canned, put artichoke hearts in strainer and wash quickly under cold running water to wash off additives.

In food processor fitted with steel blade, place butter around blades. With motor running, add flour through feed tube. Process until mixture is smooth.

Bring milk to boil. Add butter-flour mixture to milk. Whisk vigorously to avoid lumps. Bring sauce to a boil. Cook over low heat 4 to 5 minutes. Whisk constantly to avoid scorching. Season with dry mustard, onion juice, salt and white pepper. Add artichoke hearts. (This much can be done ahead.)

Remove dish from heat; add beaten egg and half of grated Swiss cheese (¼ cup). Stir until blended.

Scatter remaining ¼ cup cheese and 2 Tablespoons bread crumbs over artichoke heart mixture and sprinkle faintly with paprika. Bake 15 minutes or until mixture bubbles.

30

Baked Cucumbers

Such a dandy, simple vegetable dish should be rescued from the faded pages of an old family cookbook, where I first discovered it, and preserved for posterity.

4 medium cucumbers*
2 medium onions,
  chopped
20 salted crackers,
  crumbed
2 Tablespoons (or more)
  sour cream
6 slices bacon, cooked
  and crumbled
⅛ teaspoon pepper,
  freshly ground

FOR THE TOPPING:
Additional 1½ salted
  crackers, crumbed
1½ Tablespoons butter
2 cans (14½-oz. each)
  chicken stock

*If cucumbers are waxed, scrub wax off under running hot water. This will improve taste no end.

Serves 8

Halve cucumbers lengthwise and scoop out pulp, but leave shells intact. (Do not peel or seed cucumbers.) Coarsely chunk cucumber pulp and place in bowl. Add onions, cracker crumbs (made either in food processor with steel blade or with a rolling pin), sour cream to bind, and crumbled bacon, with a few grinds of peppermill. Mix together.

Divide and spoon mixture into cucumber shells. Sprinkle with additional cracker crumbs for topping and dot with butter. Place in broiler pan surrounded by chicken stock. Bake 40 minutes. Serve warm. Urge your guests to be sure to eat the cucumber skin. Very healthful.

Other Old-Time Recipes from Denver's Bygone Days

Beaten Biscuits

Certainly no recipe personifies our heritage from the Deep South more than Beaten Biscuits. To me, they signify an endless holiday groaning board where they are usually accompanied by slivers of ham. In olden days, that ham was always a Smithfield ham, but today, since its price has soared to incredible heights, the Smithfield ham has been replaced by a Missouri ham, or even one less expensive.

What remains the same is twofold. The whole ham should always be presented on a buffet table, but the carving of the parchment-like slices of ham should be started. Only the whole ham gives such a sumptuous effect.

The other holdover is the appeal beaten biscuits enjoy. Admittedly, it would be more pleasurable to still have some cook in the kitchen making them for you, kneading them forever, and either pulling the dough through some roller or pounding it with a mallet endlessly. But that is a pipe dream.

Once you have tasted Beaten Biscuits with a sliver of ham inside, you can never be happy with any other kind of cracker or biscuit. So when it is cold and snowy outdoors and you are searching for a kitchen project, this recipe for Beaten Biscuits will involve you for several hours. Remember I warned you of the time involved but don't let me scare you away from the fun of making them. Once you have made Beaten Biscuits, simply store them in a cookie tin and they will last indefinitely (if little hands stay out of the cookie tin).

I have left this fourth-generation recipe unspoiled except for the new-fangled technique of folding dough in half and making two layers. Our grandmothers would have frowned on this addition.

4 cups unsifted, unbleached flour
1 teaspoon salt
1½ Tablespoons sugar
4 oz. shortening (measure by pouring 4 oz. cold water in measuring cup and then adding shortening until water mark is 8 oz.)
⅜ cup cold milk
⅜ cup ice water

One cookie sheet, ungreased

FOR GLAZE:
2 Tablespoons melted butter

Yield: makes about fifty 1¾" biscuits (recipe can be halved)

Into food processor bowl fitted with steel blade, put dry ingredients. Add cut up shortening (not in blobs). Process until mixture is like coarse meal. With motor running, through feed tube, pour gradually the milk-ice water mixture. Dough should be stiff. Remove dough to a lightly floured board.

Here is where the fun begins. You must knead the dough for a minimum of ten minutes. If dough is too bulky, divide it in half.

Put dough through any roller available in your kitchen. (The optimum is a beaten biscuit table, complete with roller, inherited by me from my great-grandmother.) If you have a machine to make pasta, it will work very well, but you may have to divide dough.

Should you have no roller in your kitchen, pound dough with a rolling pin or mallet.

Whatever technique you use, rolling or pounding, dough must be rolled or beaten a minimum of 100 times until it is well blistered.

Preheat oven to 325°.

After dough becomes smooth and glossy, roll dough out on a lightly floured surface to make a rectangle (1/8"-1/4" thick). You may have to do this several times. Fold dough in half to form two layers. With a biscuit cutter or rim or small glass, cut biscuits and place on cookie sheet(s). Brush tops lightly with melted butter. With fork tines, prick tops of biscuits several times. Place sheets in oven. Bake at least 30 minutes. Check doneness by opening one biscuit to see if dough is cooked through. If necessary, add additional baking time. Biscuits should be very hard.

Remove cookie sheet(s) from oven. Let biscuits cool. Place biscuits, layered with waxed paper, in cookie tin to store.

Other Old-Time Recipes from Denver's Bygone Days

Creamed Hominy

This southern traditional grain dish is a great accompaniment for a Colorado cookout with a steak or barbecued chicken.

1½ cups hominy
1½ Tablespoons butter
Salt and pepper, freshly
  ground, to taste
1½ cups cream

Serves 8

Heat hominy in water it was cooked in or liquid from can. Drain and add butter, salt and pepper to taste. Add cream. Cook mixture slowly, until very hot and blended.

A word about hominy: hominy is corn with the hull and grain removed. Hominy can be dried and ground into coarse flour for baking, cooked as a cereal, or used in any recipe calling for corn. Hominy grits—also called corn grits-are the broken grains.

If you are ambitious to eat wisely and into grains, make your own hominy with dried corn and baking soda—a process taking 15 hours. Best of luck.

Cucumber Mint Mayonnaise

Another pearl in a dazzling old-time Denverite's repertoire. Delightful when served to embellish a dish of fish, served cold, or any shellfish salad.

One medium-size cucumber,
  peeled (European cucumber*
  preferable)
1 cup mayonnaise
  (made with your favorite
  recipe)
1 Tablespoon fresh mint
  leaves, finely chopped
  (use scissors)

*European cucumbers are elongated and have fewer seeds. Look for them in your local market.

Yield: about 1½ cups

Put peeled cucumber, chunked, around steel blade of food processor and process briefly. Scrape sides of bowl downward, and process again briefly. Reserve.

To one cup homemade mayonnaise, add finely chopped cucumber and finely chopped mint leaves. Serve well chilled.

Gertrude's Sour Cream Dressing

This recipe, which crossed state borders, is from an old-time family cookbook in my paternal family. Delightfully simple to make and simply delightful to taste.

⅛ Tablespoon onion juice
¾ cup sour cream
  (or yogurt)
Salt and white pepper
  to taste
Juice of ½ lemon
½ teaspoon sugar or
  ¼ teaspoon honey (optional)

Yield: about ¾ cup
Combine all ingredients in bowl (never food processor) to make a delicious dressing. This recipe is enough to dress 2 cups shredded cabbage or lettuce.

Variations include using chives or any fresh garden herb instead of onion juice. A wee bit of sugar or honey may be added for a hint of sweetness. Yogurt (⅜ cup) can be substituted for sour cream to make a lighter low-cal dressing.

Other
Old-Time
Recipes
from
Denver's
Bygone
Days

Mehlman Dressing

Since this recipe was originated by a whiz cook and longtime manager of a prominent Denver country club, many Denverites consider this recipe IMMORTAL!

2 cups mayonnaise
2 medium-ripe avocados,
  mashed
1 Tablespoon Dijon mustard
1 Tablespoon vinegar
Juice of half lemon*
2 Tablespoons sugar *or*
  1 Tablespoon plus
  1 teaspoon honey
  (optional)
1 Tablespoon grated onion
Salt and white pepper
  to taste

Yield: about 2⅓ cups
Combine all ingredients in food processor fitted with steel blade or in blender. Process until mixed, just short of puréeing. Refrigerate in jar with tight-fitting lid. This dressing will keep indefinitely in refrigerator.

*Use this old trick when only a small amount of lemon juice is needed: wrap lemon in corner of kitchen towel, and squeeze out juice. No seeds nor pulp emerges and very little mess.

Peanut Brittle over Ice Cream

This recipe is a Denver transplant. I have such indelible memories of the long family table presided over by my grandparents where this favored dessert was often a part of the ritual. When it was not served, we children demanded it. So, bet your bottom dollar such a family jewel was brought to Denver by me as a bride.

1 lb. peanut brittle
2 qts. French vanilla
  ice cream

Serves 8

Place ice cream in your best serving bowl and crumble peanut brittle pieces on top. What could be easier?

Snow Squares with Butter Sauce

An amusing and unforgettable culinary memory of mine: I was concocting this dessert the day before our family Thanksgiving Feast, and simultaneously, a local newspaper was photographing, in color, a group of us in my home to promote a local charity. Thus, I was unavoidably cornered more than half an hour—the ideal beating time to create Snow Squares. Rushing back to my kitchen, to my horror, I discovered the ceiling plastered with gobs of meringue, so had no choice but to repeat the whole recipe. Have you ever had to make a recipe twice? But it was well worth it because this extravagant dessert remains a family favorite of ours and many old-time Denverites, who count on serving it in any season.

1 package unflavored
  gelatin
4 Tablespoons cold water
1 cup boiling water
⅔ cup superfine sugar
3 egg whites
¼ teaspoon salt
1 teaspoon vanilla
16 graham crackers,
  crumbed very fine

One oblong glass pan,
  approximately 9″ × 13½″

Serves 8

Sprinkle gelatin over cold water in mixer bowl. Let soak 5 minutes. Add boiling water and sugar. Stir until dissolved. Let cool slightly. Add unbeaten egg whites, salt and vanilla.

Beat at high speed until mixture is light and resembles thick cream (about 30 minutes). Mixture should have no bubbles. Turn into pan and chill until firm.

To serve: with sharp knife, divide into three sections horizontally. Then cut into 1″ squares (about 24). Roll each Snow Square in graham cracker crumbs. Serve each guest three squares napped with this lavish Butter Sauce.

Beat egg yolks until thick and lemon-colored. Gradually add sugar. Continue to beat while adding butter, lemon zest and juice. Fold in lightly whipped cream and chill Butter Sauce.

FOR THE BUTTER SAUCE:
4 egg yolks
⅔ cup superfine sugar
6 oz. unsalted butter,
  melted
2 Tablespoons lemon zest,
  grated
4 Tablespoons lemon juice
⅔ cup heavy cream,
  lightly whipped

Golden Gossamer Wafers

This is not a recipe for a novice cook — rather it should be any cook's aspiration. As I have enjoyed these heavenly wafers since my childhood, they remain my favorite cookies of all time. Make them when you have a free unharried day, as they are well worth the extra trouble. Everyone gobbles them up as if he will never again have another in his lifetime. Golden Gossamer Wafers: my vision of Paradise.

4 oz. unsalted butter,
   cut up
1 cup powdered sugar,
   sifted
½ teaspoon vanilla
1¾ cups (6 oz.) cake flour,
   sifted
½ cup milk
½ teaspoon cinnamon
½ teaspoon ginger

One cookie sheet, lightly
   buttered and chilled

Makes about 100 extra-thin wafers

Preheat oven to 325°.

In food processor fitted with steel blade, place cut up butter and process briefly. Measure sifted powdered sugar to obtain 1 cup. Add sugar through feed tube of food processor with motor running. Process until mixture is smooth. Add vanilla and process briefly.

Weigh on kitchen scales or measure sifted cake flour. Measure by dipping ½ cup measure into flour and leveling with a knife. Repeat until all flour is used. Resift. Add cake flour alternately with milk to butter-sugar mixture in food processor bowl. Add spices. Process until integrated.

Using a wide spatula, spread about 2 Tablespoons of the mixture evenly over the entire cookie sheet. This operation has to be performed with great care and patience to cover any potential holes or ragged ends of dough on cookie sheet. Try to spread the dough as thin as possible, yet have it fully cover the cookie sheet. With a sharp knife, mark off dough into 1½" squares. Bake wafers about 6 to 7 minutes until they attain a very light golden sheen.

Remove cookie sheet from oven, and while wafers are hot, quickly cut again through marked squares with knife. Slip a small spatula underneath to remove wafers and allow them to cool on a platter. Repeat process over and over until all dough is used. Keep wafers stored in a tin—in layers and carefully separated with wax paper. Hope they last long enough at your house to store!

Other
Old-Time
Recipes
from
Denver's
Bygone
Days

Culinary Denver In Transition

A recent headline in *The Denver Post* tells us that Denver has the fourth busiest airport in the world! Certainly every Denverite was rocked by this bulletin. "Fourth Busiest" refers to the number of airplane landings and take-offs daily, but Stapleton International Airport is also the seventh busiest in the world when judged only by the head count—of both commercial and private passengers.

Beginning as nothing but a vast prairie a half-century ago, Denver's airport and its meteoric growth, capsulizes what has happened to the city and its inhabitants in this same time span. After years of building Denver, its citizens in all walks of life now sally forth to the four corners of the globe and, conversely, entertain guests from all over the world in today's Denver.

As the bridge from the past to the present is crossed in the Mile High City, repercussions in regard to food preparation in Denver restaurants and home kitchens are manifold. Because of its isolated location on the map, Denver is insular, and because of prolonged cold winter temperatures, and an abbreviated growing season, very few food items can be raised in the city or its environs.

So there must be flown daily into Denver food such as fresh fish, caught on both coasts, and gorgeous fruit and vegetable produce, raised anywhere the best is cultivated. Refrigerated trains, which used to bring produce and all food stuffs to Denver, are just another shelved memory of many of the old-timers.

As the gateway between the Eastern and Western parts of the United States, Denver has become a melting pot of every known culture. With the result that, what we eat in Denver, whether in restaurants or at home, represents innumerable ethnic cuisines either singly or more likely, as mixtures of several types. This food, however, when well prepared and presented, always has a special Denver touch.

Another outgrowth of living in our thriving city is that as Denverites have taken to the skyways and byways of the world, they have returned to their kitchens with terrific new food ideas. No longer are they content with mediocre food. Rather, they are willing to search for and collect new recipes, which will be made from scratch and with fresh ingredients, whenever possible.

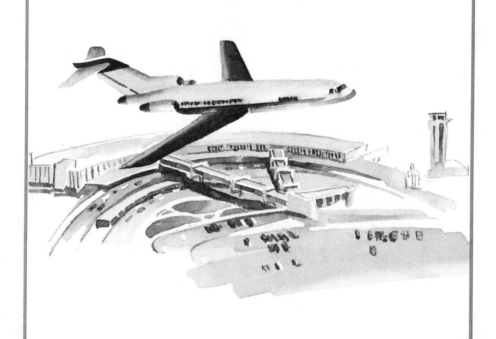

Part II

Cooking for Denver Today

Picnics and Backyard Frolics
(Alias Barbecues)

Chapter IV

Advice on Picnics and Backyard Frolics

Why does food always taste better when consumed outdoors? The main reason appetites soar is because we all become free spirits with Mother Nature, temporarily abandoning life's stresses and problems.

Eating al fresco (in the open air) is a welcome respite from the rut of ordinary meals indoors, a proven escape hatch from day in, day out family cooking and dining. So, for cooks and diners alike, the flair and imagination of the one who plans the picnic menu must be ignited and inspired. This is the first step.

Even if you don't have the time or the inclination to cook up a storm, you can still assemble a fine picnic feast for your family and friends. Should your group be attending a concert at Red Rocks, or the opera at Central City, carting along a picnic to eat before the event is far easier on the nerves and digestions of the diners than rushing into an over-crowded restaurant with all eyes on the clock. Besides, it's an opportunity to see the countryside in all its glory, as well as promoting a benignly relaxing state for the picnickers. For the host, the cost of the picnic is far easier on the shrinking pocketbook.

But if picnicking and communing with nature turn you off, you can serve a comparable dinner right in your private outside space—whether dinner is served on your apartment balcony, patio or even right on the grass (strewn with quilts or blankets) in your backyard.

The main difference between picnic food and food served in your backyard is that the former must be transportable. It has to survive the rigors of bumping along dirt roads until the host finds the perfect place to picnic (unless he has a longtime favorite). Of course, this milieu must be as far as possible from civilization, and, hopefully, near a babbling mountain stream.

Very important for safety and to avoid food poisoning, always pack foods that keep well, or use an insulated carrier. To avoid the danger zone in which bacteria can flourish (50°-125°), keep cold foods really cold and hot foods hot. All cold foods should be kept in a cooler with plenty of ice. Return any leftovers to cooler immediately.

Dining in your private outdoor space, however, has some advantages. The most important difference between picnicking and dining in your own backyard is that when hosting a picnic elsewhere, you must remember everything, or you and your guests are out of luck. To help you pack your picnic basket flawlessly, so you won't forget one item, consult my Picnic Basket Check List. Also my ardent advice is to write out your complete menu, with accompanying drinks, and cross each item off as you pack it into the picnic basket.

Well do I recall hosting a picnic miles from civilization when, to my horror, I discovered futilely that the divine salad I had painstakingly prepared was equally miles away, lodged in our home refrigerator. Maybe you've had a comparable experience—perhaps discovering a corkscrew was forgotten when bottles of chilled white wine were just to be opened. Incidentally, one person alone should be responsible for packing the picnic basket, along with other picnic necessities of my picnic basket check list, as two cooks can too easily blame each other for anything left out.

42

When frolicking in your backyard: if you forget anything, it's simple to obtain it quickly from your own kitchen. Another crucial point in favor of dining in the backyard is that you have the fun and sheer delight of barbecuing without the struggle of making a fire from scratch in the woods. Though some picnickers have been steeped in Boy Scout training, never count on it. Countless picnics have become unmitigated disasters because of crummy fires. Far better for the host/ hostess to provide easy-to-serve already-cooked food.

Barbecuing in the backyard is comparatively simple today with a handy gadget to light the coals. Lacking that, pour a little (watch it carefully!) kerosene over the coals to alight them effortlessly. In Colorado where weather is ever-changing, a cover for the barbecue saves undue strain on the cook's nerves.

Of course, if you can seduce the usual non-cook of the host team to perform the barbecue ritual, this sharing of responsibilities simplifies everything for the chief cook. Since guests make a beeline to gather around the grill with its attendant chef, the barbecuer can bask in glory as the food is inspected, judged and cooked to perfection.

One small but vital admonition: always spray vegetable oil on grills used for food to be barbecued. This makes the post-meal cleanup far less odious, as well as preventing the food, as it is cooking, from sticking to the grill. (Fish is the worst sinner in this regard.)

Another hint: when barbecuing meat, try to turn it only once during cooking to avoid losing juice on the topside as it cooks. Also, always turn meat with a pair of tongs or spatula instead of a fork to avoid piercing. Remember to salt meat only after cooking; and, preferably, let each diner salt his own to his taste.

When devising a tasty barbecue menu, in addition to your barbecued entree try to have at least one other hot dish. Serve everything else cold, if you wish.

Because, especially in summer, Denver attracts an unending stream of friends who arrive from all over the world, we need picnics and backyard frolics as easy and simple formats for entertaining. Both of them are amusing outdoor sports which spontaneously become contagious sporting outdoor amusements, where an instant camaraderie develops among guests.

Picnics and Backyard Frolics
(Alias Barbecues)

These varied menus, hopefully will give you inspiration and can be a springboard for you to concoct your own menu, remembering to include ingredients at their seasonal prime. This practice will save you money and ensure your serving forever the best and the freshest.

All starred recipes are included in **Denver Delicious**.

A Volkswagen Picnic

Easy, reasonable and for feeding a small crowd.

Gazpacho*

Selection of Ready-Made Sausage from the Deli
(Such as a Cheese and Salami Loaf, Summer Sausage, Polish Sausage or Smoked Italian or German Sausage)

Chinese Crystal Chicken with Broth*

Selection of Cheese from the Deli
(For instance; Jarlsberg, Danish Fontina, Danish Crème Havarti, String Cheese, Alouette or Rondele)

Pickles and Olives

Fresh Fruits in Season

Long Baguettes of French Bread

Orange Poppy Seed Cake*

Fruit Juice or Beer
or
Jug California Gamay Beaujolais

A Chevrolet Picnic

Inexpensive, but takes a bit more time to prepare (you can prepare this picnic in steps over several days), and, naturally, plan for a few more guests than the Chevrolet accommodates. All my recipes are for eight servings to provide for those extra guests.

Chilled Curried Zucchini Soup*

Scotch Eggs* **

Vegetable Pâté* or Stuffed Whole Artichokes*
(Cold Baby Artichokes may be substituted)

Cooked Cabbage Salad with Yogurt
and Caraway Seed Dressing* **

Very Lemon Bread*

5-3 Ice* or Watermelon

Tried-and-True Chocolate Chip Cookies*

Jug Beaujolais Villages '79
or
Fruit Juice or Beer

**Actually, only the Scotch Eggs and Cooked Cabbage Salad with Yogurt and Caraway Seed Dressing have to be prepared the day of the picnic. Everything else may be prepared ahead.

Porsche Picnic for Lovers

Only a twosome fits comfortably into a Porsche, so this tête-à-tête might occur at an outdoor mountain retreat near a bubbling stream. This picnic, like a Porsche, is on the chi-chi side, racy and sportive.

Wolfgang's Cucumber Soup*

Colorado Cornish Pasties*

Slimming Vegetables à la Grecque*
or Crudités
(fresh vegetable sticks in your favorite dunk)

Pickles and Olives

Plugged Melon*

Brandy Snaps*

Pinot Chardonnay
or
Macon Villages 1976

Cadillac Picnic

Here is a picnic for those who have made it in this world or intend to. It is classy, chic and elegant. This menu is more trouble for the cook to prepare, yet well worth the extra trouble.

Hot Clam Consommé with Sherry*

Green Peppercorn Pâté*

Fettuccine Fling with Cold Tomato Sauce*

Stuffed Whole Artichokes* or Wild Rice Salad*

Quick Herbed Onion Bread*

Fresh Peach Ice Cream*

Brandy Snaps*

Korbel Brut Champagne
or
Lanson Champagne

Station Wagon Tailgate Picnic

Remember that my other car menus can easily be adapted for a tailgate picnic. A tailgate picnic is comparable to a small buffet, since it is usually served from a pseudo-table at the back end of the station wagon, where guests stand around, sipping and munching. Very often a tailgate picnic precedes an athletic event like a football or soccer game, so the menu should be controlled and casual.

Hot Bloody Mary Soup*

Pita Bread Sandwiches Stuffed with Tabbouleh*
and Topped with Alfalfa Sprouts

Oriental Stuffed Chicken Drumsticks*
or Slices of Roast Beef

Fettuccine Fling with Cold Tomato Sauce*

Cold Stuffed Zucchini Boats*

Green Tomato and Apple Pie with Pastry Crusts*

Jug California Gamay Beaujolais
or
Fruit Juice or Beer

Volkswagen Backyard Frolic

Here your car stays in your driveway. Because you are so near your kitchen, it is easy to serve two or more hot foods. Also, your trusty charcoal grill is ready with coals to be lit.

Gazpacho*

Charcoal-Grilled Chickens**

Corn on the Cob***

Green Salad with Broadmoor's Ginger Cream Dressing*

Heated Long Baguettes of French Bread

Orange Poppy Seed Cake*
or Fresh Fruit in Season

California Dry Chablis
or
Iced Mint Tea

**Grill chickens, previously marinated in vegetable oil with lemon juice, to their ultimate degree of flavor. Their hallmark will be a crust of an exquisite brown color.

***Also roasted in husks on grills.

Chevrolet Backyard Frolic

This picnic might be for neighbors. Also, it would be an ideal picnic for a dinner club where each couple brings one ready-made dish. Even if you don't belong to such a club, this sharing of the preparation is a smart idea.

Cold Curry Cream Soup*

Cornhusk Trout Barbecued*
or Velma's Barbecued Spareribs*

Fried Rice* or Corn Grilled in Husks

Tropical Bananas*

Sliced Beefsteak Tomatoes

Quick Herbed Onion Bread*

5-3 Ice* or Watermelon

Tried-and-True Chocolate Chip Cookies*

Taylor's Hearty Red Burgundy
or
California Côtes du Rhône

Porsche Backyard Frolic for Lovers

Here is a perfect menu to entertain and feed your heart-of hearts. Three is definitely a crowd for this picnic.

Israeli Avocado Soup Cold*

Grilled Filets of Beef

Fettuccine Fling with Cold Tomato Sauce*

or

Potatoes Baked in Coals**

Sliced Beefsteak Tomatoes

Pickles

Pineapple-on-a-Spit*
(if you have rôtisserie)

or

Plugged Melon*
(Casaba, Honeydew or Persian)

Pecan Moons*

California Jordan Cabernet Sauvignon

**Simply bury scrubbed potatoes in coals. Bake 45 to 60 minutes, depending on their size. When a fork can easily pierce potatoes, they are done. Overlook the blackness of the skin, as the insides will be marvelously tender and flaky.

Cadillac Backyard Frolic

Can't you see this driveway lined with the host couple's Cadillac and another Cadillac or two of the guests? All big spenders who have earned it the hard way. We hope.

Hot Bloody Mary Soup*

**Grilled Salmon Steaks
or Shrimp-on-Skewer**
(with onions and green peppers)

Wild Rice Salad*

Asparagus Mousse*

Honeyed Beer Bread*

Fresh Peach Ice Cream*

Brandy Snaps*

**California Schramsberg Blanc de Noir
Champagne**

Check List for Picnic Basket

To save last minute hassles and to help the cook-and-picnic-packer's frazzled nerves, it is wise to leave the picnic basket fully packed with as many of the essentials as you can spare. Of course, after the post-picnic clean up, brush out the basket so it is tidy. If necessary, wash or clean any dirty item before storing it in your basket.

Basket Essentials (For the picnic site)

Bags for trash
Binoculars
Camera and film
Coffee pot
Corkscrew with bottle opener
Cutting board
First aid equipment
Flashlight
Insect repellent
Knives (bread, carving and small paring knives, at least)

> For safety in storing and/or transporting knives, place point of each knife blade in a discarded wine cork.

Moist disposable towelettes
Napkins
Roll of paper towels, a box of tissues and a roll of toilet paper
Sun lotion
Tablecloth

If you are Making a Fire or Warming a Dish

Extra newspaper
Hot pads
Kerosene
Matches (stored in a waterproof plastic bag)
Pans
Sterno

Picnic Essentials to Carry Outside of Basket

Blankets and/or quilts
Food cooler
Food warmer
Sun hats
Sweaters

For the Table (Whether Dining on the Ground or at a Table)

Flatware
Plates
Serving utensils (large spoons, fork, salad spoon and fork)
Soup mugs

For the Food

Butter
Jelly or jam
Pickles or relish
Salt and pepper

For the Drinks

Cream and sugar
Ice
Lemons and limes
Non-alcoholic fruit juices, carbonated beverages (including mixes)
Tea and/or coffee
Water glasses or cups
Water in jug (enough to put out fire?)
Wine glasses (preferably stemmed and unbreakable)

Chilled Curried Zucchini Soup

This soup poured from a thermos during a picnic or at a backyard frolic (with chilled soup bowls and the garnish), evokes a fresh-from-the-garden taste to whet appetites. When guests taste it, they are never disappointed.

6 Tablespoons butter
3-4 (about 2 lbs.) zucchini,
  chopped
1 cup scallions with
  tops, minced
1 Tablespoon curry powder
1 Tablespoon ground cumin
2 cups chicken stock
  (reserve ¼ cup)
3 cups buttermilk
Salt and white pepper
  to taste

GARNISH (optional):
½ carrot
Additional ½ zucchini
2 radishes

Serves 8

Melt butter in pan over moderate heat. Add zucchini and scallions. Cover mixture with a buttered round of wax paper and lid and cook 15 minutes, or until zucchini is soft. Remove lid and wax paper. Season vegetables with curry powder and ground cumin, previously dissolved in ¼ cup chicken stock. Cook mixture an additional 2 minutes, as you stir constantly. Pour in remaining chicken stock and continue stirring.

In food processor bowl fitted with steel blade, place zucchini mixture to purée. Add buttermilk gradually through feed tube. Process swiftly to mix. Add salt and white pepper. Process swiftly. Pour into large bowl or pitcher. Chill soup for at least four hours. If you wish, soup can be made the day before. Serve in chilled bowls.

If you want an eye-catching garnish, slice carrot and zucchini on the diagonal and slice radishes thinly. Chill these vegetables in iced water at least one hour. Garnish each soup bowl with these chilled vegetables.

Picnics
and
Backyard
Frolics
(Alias Barbecues)

Gazpacho

Its very name conjures up all the traditions of Spanish culture, like the magnetic flamenco dancers with their castanets. Gazpacho, though, is on the other side of the Spanish spectrum with its bewitching combination of so fresh vegetables, so good for you.

Should the decreasing of calories and fats be important to you, simply omit the olive oil. You will still serve an easy-to-make soup, and tasty, particularly when tomatoes are at their prime.

On a picnic, serve Gazpacho directly from the thermos without any of the garnishes, but for a backyard caper, the garnishes served in small separate bowls, like condiments for a curry, make this healthy soup ritzy, too.

1-2 cloves garlic, peeled, coarsely chopped
2 medium tomatoes (about 1 lb.), chunked
½ large cucumber, peeled, chunked
1 bunch scallions with tops, coarsely chopped, or 1 medium onion, chunked (reserve 2 Tablespoons)
¾ large green pepper, membrane and seeds removed, chunked
2 cans (12 oz.-each) tomato juice
¼ cup olive oil
¼ cup red wine vinegar
1 teaspoon salt
¼ teaspoon pepper, freshly ground
⅛-¼ teaspoon Tabasco

GARNISH: (optional)
Remaining ½ cucumber, peeled, diced
Remaining ¼ green pepper, diced
Reserved 2 Tablespoons scallions or onion, minced
¼ cup alfalfa sprouts
3 Tablespoons chives

Serves 8
Yield: 6 cups

Into food processor bowl fitted with steel blade, place garlic cloves around blades. With motor running, process until minced. Add tomatoes (no need to peel), cucumber, scallions or onion and green pepper and process. Stop just short of puréeing so that some texture will be retained. With motor running, pour one can of tomato juice, olive oil and red wine vinegar through feed tube. Process to mix. Pour mixture into large bowl or pitcher. Stir in second can of tomato juice and seasonings. Refrigerate.

If serving garnish, place diced cucumber and green pepper and minced onion each in a separate serving bowl. Cover each dish with plastic wrap. Refrigerate.

Just before serving Gazpacho: from a thermos, shake like fury to mix again. From a soup tureen: stir to mix just before serving to blend thoroughly. Sprinkle alfalfa sprouts and scatter chives for color on top of each soup mug.

Hot Bloody Mary Soup

What better idea on a chilly day, perhaps commencing a tailgate picnic, than to have your Bloody Mary served hot? This soup is especially spicy, and if that doesn't grip you, the vodka will. Of course, teetotallers may have theirs without vodka and still enjoy a most unusual soup.

2 (6-oz.) cans Bloody Mary Mix
14 oz. tomato juice
2 (13-oz.) cans red consommé madrilène
4 drops Worcestershire sauce
4 drops Tabasco
2 tomatoes, peeled, diced
Juice of clove garlic (use garlic press)
Salt and pepper, freshly ground, to taste

BEFORE SERVING:
1 oz. vodka in each soup mug or cup

Serves 8-10

Combine liquids with tomatoes and seasonings in medium-size pan. Cook over medium heat about 15 to 20 minutes. Pour hot into preheated thermos or serve hot in soup mugs.

Just before serving, pour 1 oz. vodka into each soup cup or mug. Then, pour hot soup over vodka.

Hot Clam Consommé with Sherry

This recipe has a lot going for it. First, it is extremely low in calories. Secondly, it can be assembled in three minutes and only needs to be heated for 15 minutes. Pour it directly, hot, into a thermos for a picnic, or refrigerate it at once and reheat it just before serving. Thirdly, it is a year-round soup, equally piquant served hot or cold in your dining room for an informal or formal party or, delightful as a treat for your family, so you see that this consommé is versatile.

As an alternative, serve Clam Consommé with Sherry, chilled, jellied, during the summer season to stun your guests.

3 cups clam juice (from 8-oz. bottles)
4 cups chicken stock
Juice of half lemon
1 teaspoon garlic (put through press)
1 drop Tabasco
¼ cup *dry* sherry

GARNISH:
About 1 Tablespoon whipped cream for each soup cup
About 1 teaspoon chives for each soup cup

Serves 8

In medium-size pan over medium heat, pour clam juice, chicken stock, lemon juice, garlic and Tabasco. Bring to a boil. Reduce heat to simmer for 10 to 15 minutes. Add dry sherry. Heat, but do not boil.

Pour hot from a thermos into bouillon cups or soup cups. If you wish, garnish with unsweetened whipped cream. Sprinkle chives on top for color.

To serve jellied: add 3 Tablespoons unflavored gelatin, previously softened in ½ cup chicken stock, reserved from the original four cups specified in the recipe. When gelatin mixture is softened, stir into heated soup to melt. Pour into bowl. Refrigerate to chill.

53

Wolfgang's Cucumber Soup

Tired of the same old recipe for cucumber soup? Try this one from a notable Denver chef for a make-ahead soup (refrigerated, will last three days). Perfect to commence a mountain picnic or to serve in your own backyard, balcony or patio.

Although this Cucumber Soup is highly seasoned, remember anything to be served cold requires a more pronounced seasoning. As you drink this soup, chilled overnight, at least, the spicy flavoring becomes more subdued.

3 medium-size cucumbers, peeled, (European seedless cucumbers, preferable)
⅔ medium-size onion, peeled, or 3 medium-size shallots, peeled
21 oz. plain yogurt
2½ Tablespoons sour cream
Salt and white pepper to taste
2 drops Tabasco
¼ teaspoon cayenne
2 teaspoons Worcestershire sauce

GARNISH:
1 teaspoon fresh or frozen chives for each soup cup

Serves 8

Slice and chop cucumbers. (Can use food processor with steel blade. Process briefly.) Mince onion or shallots. (Can use food processor with steel blade. Process briefly.) Place in large bowl. With rubber spatula, fold in yogurt and sour cream carefully. Add seasonings. Blend well. Chill overnight.

To serve: Garnish each filled cold soup cup with chives.

Chinese Crystal Chicken with Broth

You have never tasted anything like this: an imaginative do-ahead picnic dish, which is also economical. Rhapsodic with a permeating Chinese seasoning combination, it is the ticket for a picnic hamper or for eating in your own backyard. Carve the whole bird in front of guests to sharpen their appetites.

The economical bonus of Chinese Crystal Chicken is the lovely broth, so be sure not to throw it out. (Pour it into a large bowl or pitcher and refrigerate it. Then, remove all the fat congealed on the top. Serve broth hot or cold on another day, not with the chicken.)

**One 4-lb. roasting
  chicken***
**12-16 thin slices fresh
  ginger root, peeled**
**Three 10-oz. cans
  chicken stock**
3 (or more) cups water
¼ cup sherry
**3 scallions with tops,
  cut up**
¼ cup celery leaves
1 teaspoon salt

One Dutch oven

Serves 8

Wash chicken well inside and out and dry thoroughly with paper towels. Remove sack with innards and neck, and any globs of chicken fat. Insert 6-8 slices fresh ginger under skin of bird.

Heat chicken stock and water in Dutch oven. Add sherry, scallions, celery leaves, remaining ginger and salt. Bring mixture to boil. Lower chicken gently into water and, if necessary, add more water until chicken is covered. Bring back to boil. Simmer, covered, 45 minutes. The aroma of this dish while cooking is most tantalizing. Remove pan from heat. Keep pan covered, and let chicken continue to cook in its contained heat an additional hour. Prick top of chicken drumstick to check that chicken is cooked throughout, with no pink or red meat.

Have nearby a large bowl of ice water with several ice cubes. Gently remove chicken from pan. Let any liquid drain off in pan. (Save broth.) Plunge chicken into ice water and immerse. Let chill 15 minutes. Drain well and place on platter. Refrigerate at least 4 hours, preferably overnight.

Before carving, remove all inserted ginger slices, as they are unpleasant to eat. If you are diet conscious, also remove chicken skin containing untold fat.

*Should your chicken be stashed away in the deep freeze, the microwave can miraculously and speedily defrost it—25 minutes at 30% power, but rotate plate of chicken three times.

Colorado Cornish Pasties

Although the original pasty (meat pie) recipe came from Cornwall, England, pasties were longtime standard fare for Colorado miners with robust appetites, particularly when they were on duty. When a miner unwrapped his lunch—a pasty—he would fondly refer to his pasty as a *"letter from home"*.

I checked out the original recipe in Cornwall to bring you back my adaptation of the real thing. Also, I discovered an amusing old Cornish saying: *"The Devil is afraid to come to Cornwall for fear of being baked into a pasty."* (I returned whole.)

The striking difference between a pasty made in Cornwall and one made in Colorado is that we cooks here prefer to dice the meat. In Cornwall, it is always sliced.

Since a Colorado Cornish Pasty enfolds meat, vegetables and some fruit, it is the entire meal. What could be more portable and easier for ideal picnic food? But remember, miners' wives did not have it easy, as the food processor has simplified, considerably, the making of pasties today. Another bonanza is that pasties can be made ahead and stashed away in the freezer, to be baked when needed.

Of course, you can vary the filling, even utilizing leftovers mixed with fresh vegetables and apples or, use fish, but omit the turnip.

FOR THE PASTRY:
3 cups unbleached flour
6 Tablespoons butter,
  chilled, cut up
6 Tablespoons margarine,
  chilled, cut up
½ cup iced water
¼ teaspoon salt

2 cookie sheets, greased

FOR THE FILLING:
3 medium potatoes
1 small onion
1 turnip (or parsnip)
8 oz. beef (loin tips,
  flank or skirt steak,
  or top of round),
  partially frozen, cut to
  fit the feed tube
Salt and pepper, freshly
  ground, to taste
1 small egg
2 apples, cored, quartered
1 teaspoon fresh lemon juice
2 Tablespoons honey
Additional 3 Tablespoons
  butter

Serves 8

Into food processor bowl fitted with steel blade, place flour. Add butter and margarine pieces around blades. Process until mixture resembles coarse bread crumbs. With food processor's motor running, pour water gradually through feed tube. Add salt. Process until dough masses. Wrap dough in plastic wrap and refrigerate for at least 30 minutes.

With food processor fitted with slicer, and with motor running, push potatoes, onion and turnip, each cut to fit through feed tube. Process to slice. Remove to another bowl. Repeat with meat and process to slice.

With meat still in food processor bowl, remove slicer and fit bowl with steel blade. (You may have to move meat around in bowl.) Process very swiftly to dice, not mince, meat. (Or, as an alternate method, slice meat with knife on cutting board. Then, dice meat slices.) Add diced meat to vegetables in bowl. Season with salt and pepper. Add beaten egg to bind.

With food processor bowl fitted with slicer, push quartered apples through feed tube and process to slice. Sprinkle apple slices with lemon juice, immediately, to preserve color, and cut in half.

Colorado Cornish Pasties continued

TO ASSEMBLE:

Divide pastry in half and roll out on a floured marble slab or cutting board. Roll pastry to about 1/8" thickness and cut four separate circles, each with an 8½" diameter. (Use plate as guide.)

Remove each circle from marble slab or cutting board and fold in half. Repeat with remaining dough (half of batter) to make three more identical semi-circles.

Repeat whole process exactly to make four additional identical circles. There will be eight circles in all.

Preheat oven to 400°.

Spread one circle flat to fill. Place about 2 Tablespoons meat mixture on right side of lower "half moon". Place about 1 Tablespoon apple pieces on left side of lower "half moon". Top apples with honey. Place one teaspoon butter over just the meat mixture. Fold over top "half moon". Wet one edge with water to seal pastry tightly. Either crimp edges tightly, using thumb and forefinger, or use a pastry roller over edges. Roll as near edge as possible. Save excess pastry. Use it to make miniature pasties for kids.

FOR THE GLAZE:
Additional 1 egg, beaten

Brush both sides of each pasty with egg glaze. Place pasties on cookie sheets. Cut two or three slashes in top of each pasty so steam can escape. Bake 20 minutes. Change cookie sheets from higher to lower racks and vice versa, for even baking. Turn oven down to 325° and bake an additional 15 to 20 minutes.

Cornhusk Trout Barbecued

This trout recipe is an absolute novel presentation, guaranteed to astound all guests with your culinary talent. In truth, preparing Cornhusk Trout is the simplest way I know to cook trout. What's more, you have no messy pans to wash afterwards.

The special flavor that cornhusks impart to trout as they are cooking is hard to define. But take my word for it: you'll never have any better cooked trout anywhere in the world.

In addition, Cornhusk Trout conserves energy if you grill an additional eight ears of corn in their husks at the same time you are barbecuing the trout. You should start grilling the corn 15 to 20 minutes earlier.

Eight (½ lb. each) cleaned
  fresh trout
4 oz. butter, softened
2 teaspoons fresh lemon juice
8 bay leaves, stems removed
Salt and pepper, freshly
  ground, to taste
1 Tablespoon marjoram
8 slices bacon
8 complete cornhusks (corn
  cobs removed, for use at a
  different time)

GARNISH:
8 lemon wedges, seeded

Serves 8

Make a paste of softened butter and lemon juice. Divide into eight portions.

Wash each trout and pat dry with paper towels. Put one portion of lemon-butter mixture into cavity of each trout. Stuff one crushed bay leaf into each cavity.

Season skin of each trout with salt, pepper and marjoram. Wrap one slice of bacon around each trout. Place trout into empty cornhusk. Wrap string around end of each cornhusk to secure trout. (It may be necessary to wrap string around in two different places.) Repeat procedure with each trout.

When charcoal has become glowing embers, place Cornhusk Trout on grill, previously sprayed with no-stick oil. Barbecue 10 to 15 minutes on each side or until fish flakes easily when tested with a fork.

Serve immediately with a dish of 8 lemon wedges in center of dining table.

Oriental Stuffed Chicken Drumsticks

Admittedly, this recipe takes some time to prepare, but it is well worth the effort for two reasons. First, Oriental Stuffed Drumsticks make an inexpensive entrée. Secondly, most of your guests will never have seen a stuffed drumstick, so will be in absolute awe of your cooking expertise.

Oriental Stuffed Chicken Drumsticks, equally succulent served hot or cold, can be beguiling for your moveable feast. Reminder: these stuffed drumsticks need to be refrigerated for at least 2 hours before sautéing them.

TO PREPARE DRUMSTICKS:
8 chicken drumsticks with thighs (second joint) attached

Serves 8

To "bone" chicken drumsticks, you actually leave the bone in, but free the meat around the bone to allow room for stuffing. With a boning or other sharp knife, cut around base of drumstick to free meat.

With knife close to bone and being careful not to pierce skin or make holes, scrape the meat towards the thigh from the end of the bone. Pull the meat inside out like a glove, in order to remove any white tendons or gristle. Replace meat over bone. Refrigerate drumsticks while preparing and cooling stuffing.

FOR THE STUFFING:
½ lb. pork, chunked
1-2 cloves garlic
4-5 scallions with tops, cut up
¼ cup fresh ginger root, peeled
1 Tablespoon peanut oil
½ teaspoon chili powder
1-2 Tablespoons soy sauce
Pepper, freshly ground, to taste

Into food processor fitted with steel blade, place pork. Process until pork is ground like hamburger. Remove and place in a medium-size bowl.

Add garlic to food processor bowl, still fitted with steel blade, and process to mince. Add scallions to bowl and process to mince. Remove to bowl with ground pork.

Change from steel blade to shredder of food processor. With motor running, push ginger root, cut to fit feed tube, through it to shred. Add to pork mixture.

Heat peanut oil over medium-high heat. When sizzling, add pork mixture and cook until meat is no longer pink. Add chili powder, soy sauce and pepper to season. Mix thoroughly. Let mixture cool completely.

(continued on next page)

TO ASSEMBLE:
Cotton string
Salt and pepper, freshly
  ground, to taste

Stuff each chicken leg with about 2 to 3 Tablespoonsful cooked pork filling. With cotton (never plastic) string, cut into 4″ lengths, tie each chicken leg firmly in two or three places. Re-form the original shape of each chicken leg, although it will be fatter. Salt and pepper, to taste, each chicken leg with attached thigh.

Refrigerate, covered with plastic wrap, at least two hours and not more than five hours.

TO SAUTÉ:
Additional ¼ cup peanut
  oil
½ cup dry sherry
1 teaspoon arrowroot
½ cup chicken stock
Additional 3 teaspoons
  soy sauce
Additional 2 teaspoons
  ginger root, peeled, minced

Heat extra large or two medium-size skillets over high heat. When very hot, add peanut oil. Add chicken drumsticks with attached thighs. Sauté over moderate heat 5 minutes on each side. Remove chicken to a platter. Add sherry to skillet and cook to deglaze pan with metal spatula. Scrape up any brown bits clinging to bottom(s) and sides of skillet(s). Stir in arrowroot dissolved in chicken stock. Mix thoroughly. Pour in soy sauce and add additional minced ginger root. Return chicken to pan and simmer, covered, 15 minutes. Serve hot or cold.

Scotch Eggs

Scotch Eggs, an enticing perennial in English pubs, and a must for tourists, are a delectable and different addition to your picnic hamper. Also, Scotch Eggs are a surprise treat when hosting a backyard frolic.

8 small eggs, hard-boiled*
2 lbs. pork sausage
2 eggs, beaten
1 cup herb-flavored bread
  crumbs (use ½ teaspoon
  thyme and 1 Tablespoon
  fresh parsley)
Oil to deep-fat fry

***Hard-boiled eggs should be immediately put into cold water after boiling to stop any further cooking and to prevent discoloration of yolks.**

Serves 8

Peel hard-boiled eggs**. Divide sausage equally into ¼ lb. portions and make round flat discs about 3½"-4" in diameter. Wrap each egg all around with sausage and press edges together to make a smooth surface. Dip each sausage-wrapped egg into beaten-egg mixture, then coat with crumbs. Heat oil in deep-fat fryer or deep pan. When sizzling, place Scotch Eggs in oil and deep fry at 350° 10 to 12 minutes.

**Peeling hard-boiled eggs is a problem to many cooks. Older eggs peel more easily. To shell hard-boiled eggs, crack shell at round end of egg where there is a little air space, to facilitate peeling. Then roll egg between palms of your hands to loosen the thin, though tough, skin from egg.

**Picnics
and
Backyard
Frolics
(Alias Barbecues)**

Vegetable Pâté

Vegetable Pâté is a winner for all vegetarians and dieters. But if you are a carnivore (meat-eater), don't deprive yourself. I highly recommend it as the main dish because it is extremely nutritive. Do not overlook its one-of-a-kind flavor.

For a picnic, Vegetable Pâté is hard to beat. For a backyard frolic, it is soothing for the cook to have a fully prepared and refrigerated dish all set to bake and serve.

4 celery stalks, leaves
  removed, chunked
1 bay leaf, crushed
1 teaspoon salt
3 zucchini (unpeeled), chunked
4 shallots or 1 small
  onion
1 small red or green pepper,
  seeded, membrane removed,
  chunked
½ cup mushrooms
2½ Tablespoons butter
1-2 cloves garlic, minced
4 eggs
1⅓ cups whipping cream
2 teaspoons tomato paste
⅛ teaspoon pepper, freshly
  ground
1 teaspoon fresh tarragon or
  ⅓ teaspoon dried tarragon

8 individual 4 oz. ramekins,
  oiled, or one metal loaf
  pan, 5½″ × 9 ″, oiled

Serves 6

Preheat oven to 350°.

Place chunked celery in pan with water to cover. Add bay leaf and ½ teaspoon salt and bring mixture to boil. Cook over medium heat 15 minutes or until celery is crisp-tender. Drain well. Reserve in a large mixing bowl.

Into food processor bowl fitted with steel blade, place chunked zucchini. Process until coarsely ground. Remove to a separate bowl. Repeat same process with shallots or onion to mince, not purée. Add to zucchini in bowl. Repeat same process with red or green pepper to mince and add to zucchini mixture in bowl.

Into food processor bowl, still fitted with steel blade, place mushrooms to process to mince. Reserve.

Melt butter in large skillet over medium heat. When sizzling, add zucchini mixture and garlic. Sauté about 3 minutes. Add minced mushrooms. Cook an additional 3 minutes or until vegetables are just tender. Drain excess liquid from pan. With paper towel, pat vegetables dry and add to reserved celery in large mixing bowl.

Into food processor bowl, still fitted with steel blade, place eggs, whipping cream and tomato paste. Season with pepper, tarragon and remaining ½ teaspoon salt. Process briefly. Pour mixture into bowl with vegetables. Mix with a plastic or wooden spoon. Pour into either individual ramekins or loaf pan. Place ramekins or pan in a large flat pan filled halfway with hot water (bain-marie). Bake about 40 minutes for individual ramekins, or until an inserted knife comes out clean. Bake

50 to 60 minutes for loaf pan. Individual ramekins may be served on individual plates, unmolded, or left in molds.

This Vegetable Pâté is enhanced by a fresh tomato sauce*. Serve the pâté warm-to-hot the first time around and the tomato sauce hot. But for leftovers, a cold Vegetable Pâté is intriguing.

*Use recipe for Cold Tomato Sauce with Fettuccine Fling, but reheat Tomato Sauce.

Velma's Barbecued Spareribs

Velma was our party and holiday cook for more than 25 years while our children were growing up. In our opinion, she was indisputably the best party cook in Denver.

Her masterpieces, however, are very difficult to put down on paper, because she was a supreme taster – a pinch of this, and a dash of that, etc. Her prize recipes were in her head. Her rotund girth was testimony to her love of eating.

It was a bleak day at our house, when, because of her failing health, she had to leave her workshop, our kitchen. The memories of her creations will linger in the memory of everyone who ever tasted her magnificent cooking.

High among her specialties was her recipe for Barbecued Spareribs. Fortunately, over the years, I took a few notes, as I left the entire barbecuing of the ribs up to her. Yours and my product will only approximate Velma's, but Barbecued Spareribs are a sensational food.

Try my recipe the first time around, and then experiment to add a pinch of this and a dash of that until it suits your taste. That's what Velma did.

**Two sides (usually about
  5 lbs. each) pork spareribs,
  all skin removed
2 teaspoons liquid smoke
2 teaspoons chili powder
Salt and pepper, freshly
  ground, to taste**

**Serves 8
(Figure at least 1 lb. for
  each person)**

Preheat oven to 350°.

Place ribs in roaster lined with foil. To precook, roast about 45 minutes to release excess fat. Pour off all melted fat. This precooking may be done ahead.

Several hours before barbecuing ribs, cover both sides with liquid smoke, chili powder, salt and pepper. Let ribs marinate at room temperature.

Light charcoal about one hour ahead of grilling ribs.

(continued on next page)

FOR THE SAUCE:
8 oz. tomato juice
¼ cup cider vinegar or
  wine vinegar
Juice of half lemon
3-4 drops Tabasco
2 Tablespoons Worcestershire
  sauce
Salt and pepper, freshly
  ground, to taste

Be sure that charcoal has turned into glowing coals. Spray racks with non-stick oil. Place ribs on racks, and lower coals underneath racks so that the grilling is slow to very slow. Combine ingredients for sauce. With a pastry brush, cover top side of ribs with sauce. Cover grill.

Caution: do not use excess liquid smoke, as it is flammable and ribs will be charred rather than barbecued. (I learned this the hard way.)

Barbecuing ribs takes a lot of tender, almost constant, care, as you must baste them at least every 15 to 20 minutes. Also, turn them occasionally to baste and cook evenly. Cook until ribs are nicely browned and deliciously glazed. Cooking time is about an hour. (The exact time depends on thickness of ribs and intensity of heat.) You must watch them as they cook. If ribs are overcooked, they become dry and tough. So do remember to baste them frequently to avoid that.

If wintry weather prevents grilling spareribs outdoors, bake them in a 350° oven and baste as described.

Artichokes Stuffed with Peas, Carrots and Ham

The center of attraction at any outdoor feast may well be stuffed artichokes. When artichoke stuffing is made of vegetables, it is far less expensive than when stuffed with fish or meat. You still achieve the same effect.

Artichokes may be stuffed and refrigerated several hours ahead of serving. Wrapped individually, nothing is more transportable.

There is something most sophisticated about eating a well-cooked artichoke and a stuffed one takes the prize.

8 artichokes
½ teaspoon salt
4 Tablespoons olive oil
2 small cloves garlic, minced
1½ Tablespoons thyme
¾ teaspoon oregano
¾ cup ham, finely diced
¾ cup carrots, finely shredded
¾ cup peas
3 scallions with tops, finely chopped
¾ cup parsley, minced
Salt and pepper, freshly ground, to taste
1 Tablespoon lemon juice
1 cup (or more) white table wine
3 cups water

Serves 8

Wash artichokes in cold water. Use a stiff brush to scrub off any brown or purple spots so artichokes are pristine green. Cut off stems and discard any extraneous leaves on stems and any outer wilted leaves. With scissors, cut off hard tips of each leaf to straighten. With sharp knife, whack off top third of artichoke (this makes stuffing and "de-fuzzing" of artichokes easier).

In a large pan of boiling salted water with 1 Tablespoon of the olive oil, place artichokes. Scald artichokes for only five minutes. Remove artichokes from water and invert (this makes removal of chokes easier and simplifies stuffing procedure) while you make the stuffing.

Over high heat in medium-size skillet, heat remaining 3 Tablespoons olive oil. When sizzling, turn heat down to medium and sauté briefly garlic with thyme and oregano. Remove pan from heat and add diced ham, carrots, peas, scallions and parsley. Mix thoroughly and add salt and pepper. Reserve.

(continued on next page)

Press down on each inverted artichoke prior to stuffing to force leaves open. Remove each fuzzy choke with a grapefruit spoon. Scrape underneath each choke to clean. Sprinkle each cavity with lemon juice to preserve color. Spoon about one Tablespoonful stuffing into each cavity. With a coffee spoon, carefully scoop one spoonful stuffing down into each leaf. Push far down. Try to distribute stuffing evenly into each leaf.

Preheat oven to 350°.

In a large roaster, place stuffed artichokes. Pour 1 cup white table wine with 3 cups water around artichokes. Cover roaster tightly. Place in oven to steam about 45 minutes. It may be necessary to add additional wine with water if liquid evaporates.

Remove artichokes from oven. Refrigerate until ready to serve. If transporting artichokes, remember to wrap each one individually in plastic wrap.

Chinese Fried Rice

The Chinese New Year greeting is *"May your rice never burn"*. What a useful word of caution, as rice has an innate tendency to burn. Thus, it has to be watched very carefully, as well as cooked over low heat. Just follow the package directions and your rice will never burn.

Chinese Fried Rice is served warm to hot and is a stick-to-the-ribs accompaniment to almost any entrée. Everyone likes it.

The rice for this dish should be fluffy and, if possible, cooked one day in advance of making this recipe. Reheat rice in top of double boiler.

4 cups hot cooked long
  grain rice (about 1½
  cups raw rice)
2 teaspoons peanut oil
½ cup scallions with tops,
  finely chopped
⅔ cup green pepper,
  finely chopped
2 Tablespoons soy sauce
½ cup beef stock

Serves 8

In large skillet, heat peanut oil until sizzling. Quickly sauté finely chopped scallions and green pepper.

Stir in hot cooked rice. (It is necessary to have cooked rice hot in order for it to absorb soy sauce and stock evenly and also so rice will not stick.) Mix thoroughly. Pour in soy sauce and beef stock and mix. Fry quickly, just until excess moisture disappears. Serve warm to hot.

To wash and make each wild rice kernel open "butterfly" fashion, see directions under recipe for Wild Rice with Almonds, page 7.

Cold Stuffed Zucchini Boats

The first time I was served this dish at a private home in Texas, I was wowed. Here is a vegetable recipe that can do double duty, as it is also the salad. Thus, a great time saver for the cook.

For a picnic, carefully wrapped in plastic wrap or foil, Cold Stuffed Zucchini Boats are eminently transportable. But, if you choose to eat them in your own backyard or at your dining table, plop them in the refrigerator and do not bother to wrap them.

8 small zucchini
2 medium-size tomatoes
3 cloves garlic, cut up
1 cup raw rice
½ cup pine nuts
4 teaspoons olive oil
4 teaspoons fresh herb of
  your choice (basil is best)

FOR THE BASTING SAUCE:
Additional 4 teaspoons
  olive oil
4 teaspoons white wine
4 teaspoons chicken stock
1½ Tablespoons fresh oregano
  or 2 teaspoons dried oregano

One large baking pan, oiled

Serves 8

With a sharp knife, cut off the top layer of each zucchini from one end to another. With a teaspoon, hollow out each zucchini to make a shell.

Stem and quarter tomatoes. Place them in medium-size pan to cook over high heat until boiling point is reached. Turn heat down to medium and simmer until most of liquid disappears. Remove pan from heat. When cool, put tomatoes with garlic into food processor fitted with steel blade. Process to purée. (Tomato seeds will magically disappear.)

Cook rice until every grain stands apart and is fluffy.

Preheat oven to 350°.

Blend rice with tomato purée, pine nuts, olive oil and minced fresh herb. Stuff each zucchini boat with rice mixture. Arrange in prepared baking pan. Place in oven.

To make basting sauce: combine olive oil, white wine, chicken stock and oregano and whisk to blend. Baste from time to time with sauce so that zucchini stuffing does not dry out. Baking time is about 40 minutes.

Remove zucchini boats from oven and refrigerate until ready to pack for picnic or to serve at home.

Green Peppercorn Pâté

This recipe is a find for all pâté devotees, because it is effortless to make. It is cooked on top of the stove without any baking but does have to be puréed, preferably in a food processor, after it is cooked.

If you have saved and frozen chicken livers, gizzards, and hearts when you have bought whole chickens, you don't have to rush out to buy costly meat. Although green peppercorns are pricey, you need only four teaspoons altogether. You will have most of the jar or can of green peppercorns left for use in other recipes or as a garnish.

Green Peppercorn Pâté is robust and smooth, with a flavor, at first, akin to nuts, until that taste yields to the more pronounced one of green peppercorns—surprisingly pleasant and mild.

Of course, Green Peppercorn Pâté is a fantastic first course, served on crisp lettuce leaves and accompanied by Melba toast, crackers or thin slices of French bread. It is dynamite as an hors d'oeuvre with pre-dinner drinks. But I'll take mine along in my picnic basket, thank you.

Don't forget to double the recipe and use a larger mold if you have more than eight guests.

2 Tablespoons butter
8 oz. (½ lb.) chicken livers, gizzards, hearts (fat and muscle removed)
½ cup mushrooms, chunked
½ cup scallions with tops, cut up
½ teaspoon salt
⅓ cup brandy
1 bay leaf
2 cloves garlic, minced
¼ teaspoon dry mustard
¼ teaspoon oregano
Additional 4 Tablespoons butter
4 teaspoons green peppercorns, drained

GARNISH:
Scallion leaves or any fresh herb (not mint)
Additional 2 teaspoons green peppercorns

A pâté crock or small (2-cup) mold

Serves 8

In skillet, melt butter over medium heat. Add chicken giblets, mushrooms and scallions. Season with salt. Sauté 5 minutes. Add brandy, bay leaf, garlic, mustard and oregano. Cover skillet and simmer about 20 minutes or until chicken giblets are barely tender. Remove bay leaf.

In food processor bowl fitted with steel blade, place chicken mixture with additional 4 Tablespoons butter. Process to purée. Remove to another bowl. Add additional salt, if necessary.

In another bowl, mash 2 teaspoons green peppercorns with fork. Add them with remaining 2 teaspoons whole green peppercorns to puréed mixture. Mix well. Pour into a crock or mold. Garnish surface of pâté with scallion leaves or fresh herbs and make a design of the additional 2 teaspoons green peppercorns, if desired. Cover with plastic wrap and refrigerate. Pâté, refrigerated, will last up to four days, but also, could be frozen.

Tropical Bananas

Although Denver is hardly the tropics, at least we can occasionally enjoy some tropical types of food. Tropical Bananas is a very spirited accompaniment when using your outdoor charcoal grill to cook the entrée. Fortunately, it is a year-round dish which can be an accompaniment to the entrée or can be the dessert, whichever you choose.

6-8 bananas
2 Tablespoons butter,
** melted**
⅓ cup molasses
2 Tablespoons (or more)
** rum**
Zest of one orange,
** grated**

GARNISH (optional):
Additional 2 Tablespoons
** rum to ignite**

One shallow casserole or
** baking dish, preferably**
** oven-to-table**

Serves 8

Preheat oven to 375°.

Peel bananas and split lengthwise. Cut into thirds or fourths or leave just halves, as you wish. Preferably in one layer, arrange bananas in casserole or baking dish.

Over bananas, pour mixture of butter, molasses and rum. Sprinkle orange zest on top.

Bake about 30 minutes. Baste two or three times with juices that have accumulated during baking. (Cooking time depends on ripeness of bananas.)

Only when serving Tropical Bananas as dessert, and if you want to show off a bit, pour additional rum (about 2 Tablespoons) over cooked bananas and ignite. Bring dish to table flaming, but be careful to watch that flames are contained in shallow dish and do not jump to anyone.

Cooked Cabbage Salad with Yogurt and Caraway Seed Dressing

Tired of the same old cole slaw? Here's a new twist for an exceptional salad, as you first boil the cabbage. Furthermore, it's a transportable salad—even with its dressing. But do toss cabbage with dressing just before you embark on a picnic, or during happy hour at picnic site. This saves frazzled nerves of the host/hostess concerned about serving a soggy salad at the picnic. Besides, whether you enjoy Cooked Cabbage Salad away from civilization or at home, you'll remember it kindly. Don't forget how good yogurt is for you, too.

**One firm cabbage
(about 2 lbs.)
1 teaspoon salt**

Serves 8

Discard any wilted outer leaves of cabbage. Quarter cabbage. Into food processor bowl fitted with steel blade*, place cabbage around blades. Process with two 10-second bursts to chop coarsely.

Fill Dutch oven or large pot with salted water and bring to boil. Add chopped cabbage and return water to boil. Cook only about 5 minutes. Drain cabbage in colander in sink, as you run cold water over it to refresh. Toss until cabbage is cool. Drain thoroughly. (Cooked cabbage can be refrigerated and used to make recipe the following day.)

*Since both food processor's slicer and shredder tend to liquidize cabbage, it is best to use steel blade.

**FOR THE YOGURT AND
CARAWAY SEED DRESSING:
1 cup plain yogurt
2 scallions including green
tops, chopped
1 teaspoon caraway seeds
1 teaspoon celery seeds
1 teaspoon dry mustard**

Yield: 1¼ cups

Into a small bowl, pour yogurt. Stir in chopped scallions. Add seasonings. With a spoon, toss to mix thoroughly. (Do not use food processor or blender.)

TO ASSEMBLE:

In salad serving bowl, combine cooked cabbage with dressing. Refrigerate. Marinate at least 30 minutes before serving. Correct seasonings.

Fettuccine Fling
with Cold Tomato Sauce

If you share my passion for pasta, here is a new and unusual way to make it. This recipe could not be easier to do and the flavor is wondrous.

This is a salad served at room temperature, rather than being chilled or served hot as fettuccine usually is. Be sure to make cold tomato sauce ahead.

Fettuccine Fling is made for picnic or backyard entertaining as it can be made several hours ahead and is completely transportable.

Personally, if I can piggily gobble this one dish whether eating al fresco or indoors, I shall smile forever.

¾ lb. fettuccine
2¼ qts. boiling water
1 teaspoon salt
2 cloves garlic, finely
  minced
⅓ cup parsley leaves,
  minced
1½ teaspoons oregano
  soaked in 1 Tablespoon
  olive oil
¾ cup olive oil (reserve
  1 Tablespoon for soaking)
3 cups Cold Tomato Sauce
  (see recipe to follow)

Serves 8

Cook fettuccine in boiling salted water (about 8 minutes after water boils). Cook until fettuccine is al dente-bitey tender. Do not overcook lest it become mushy. Drain in colander under cool running water, if you wish.

Mix garlic, parsley, oregano and olive oil. Add immediately to fettuccine. Toss gently but thoroughly coat with reserved olive oil. Let mixture cool completely, but do not refrigerate.

**FOR THE COLD
  TOMATO SAUCE:**
2½ cups tomato pulp,
  chopped*
Additional 1 clove garlic,
  finely chopped
¼ teaspoon sage
Additional ½ teaspoon salt
½ teaspoon pepper, freshly
  ground

In pan over low heat, place tomato pulp with seasonings to simmer. Cook as you stir from time to time until thickened. Remove from heat. Cool.

Into food processor bowl fitted with steel blade, pour tomato sauce and process to purée. Remove to separate bowl and refrigerate. (This tomato sauce may be used with other dishes, also.)

(continued on next page)

FOR THE GARNISH:
Additional 3 Tablespoons
parsley, minced

TO SERVE FETTUCCINE FLING:

Make a well in center of fettuccine in salad bowl and fill with Cold Tomato Sauce. Garnish Tomato Sauce with additional minced parsley. Mix at picnic site or at table.

Variation: for colorful change, try spinach noodles instead of fettuccine.

*A very good trick when garden tomato population is exploding is to pick (or buy) several dozen. Stem them, but do not peel. Put them in Dutch oven or any heavy pan. Cover and let them cook down slowly over low heat, as juice evaporates. Put into plastic containers and deep freeze. Use as needed, during winter and spring, when store-bought tomatoes are apt to taste like nothing.

Slimming Vegetables à la Grecque

If you are tired of serving and eating crudités, here is a welcome alternative to those sticks of fresh vegetables. "A la Grecque" usually means the vegetables are almost floating in caloric oil, but this recipe is designed to keep you and your guests trim and ready for any Colorado sport.

Furthermore, it is not necessary to stick rigidly to my vegetable selections and amounts. You can even use up some tired vegetables in your refrigerator. This is a great way to revive them.

FOR THE MARINADE:
1½ cups chicken stock
½ cup minus 1 Tablespoon
  dry white wine
6 peppercorns
1 teaspoon thyme
6 parsley sprigs
1 bay leaf
2½ Tablespoons lemon juice
1 Tablespoon salad oil
  (safflower or peanut)

FOR THE VEGETABLES:
2 medium onions, quartered
1 medium zucchini, unpeeled,
  stemmed
1 medium green pepper,
  stemmed, membrane and
  seeds removed
1 medium sweet red pepper,
  stemmed, membrane and
  seeds removed
2 celery stalks, chunked
1 turnip, chunked
5 strips pimiento

GARNISH:
Additional 4 Tablespoons
  parsley, chopped

Serves 8

Combine all marinade ingredients in a medium pan. Bring to a boil. Cover and simmer 30 minutes. Strain through sieve.

Into food processor bowl fitted with slicer, through feed tube add onions and process to slice. Remove to separate bowl. Cut zucchini, green pepper and sweet red pepper to fit feed tube. Process swiftly to slice. Push chunked celery and turnip through feed tube to slice. Dice pimiento with knife and add to food processor bowl.

Return strained marinade to pan over heat and add onions. Cover and simmer until onions are tender. Add remaining vegetables except parsley garnish. Cover. Cook an additional 5 minutes. Pour into shallow dish. Cover and refrigerate overnight.

Serve chilled in individual small bowls or ramekins, with parsley garnish.

Tabbouleh

Originally, Tabbouleh came from Lebanon. It has travelled far and wide ever since and can easily travel to your picnic site or to your own backyard.

The most important point is that it **must** be made at least 24 hours ahead and refrigerated. Don't you hate recipes that tell you that at the very end, just as you are all set to serve?

My recipe is a unique adaptation, as you do not have to soak the cracked wheat (bulgar), nor do you need to cover it with water. It will soften and expand as the combination of the olive oil and lemon juice with the moisture from the vegetables works its minor miracle. Try it for yourself and be properly astounded.

As a variation, stuff pockets of pita bread with Tabbouleh or, eat it with your fingers, using pita bread as a scoop.

¾ cup cracked wheat
  (bulgar) - no mixes
⅓ cup olive oil
¼-⅓ cup fresh lemon juice
1 small bunch scallions
  with tops, coarsely chopped
3 stalks celery, leaves
  removed, chunked
2 tomatoes (unnecessary to
  skin if using food processor)
1 large green pepper,
  membrane and seeds removed
1 large cucumber, peeled
¾ cup parsley leaves
¾ cup mint leaves
1 teaspoon salt
Pepper, freshly ground,
  to taste
Lettuce leaves

Serves 8-10

In deep glass bowl (use inexpensive one from florist if taking salad on a picnic), pour in cracked wheat. In small measuring cup, whisk together olive oil and lemon juice and pour over cracked wheat.

Into food processor bowl fitted with steel blade, place scallions around blades. Process swiftly to finely chop. Layer over cracked wheat mixture in salad bowl. Add celery to food processor bowl and process to chop. Layer celery over scallions.

Change to slicer of food processor and cut tomatoes to fit feed tube. Process to slice. Layer over celery. Cut green pepper to fit feed tube and process to slice. Layer over tomatoes. Cut cucumber to fit feed tube and process to slice as thinly as possible. Layer over green pepper.

Using either scissors or food processor fitted with steel blade, mince parsley and mint. Sprinkle over top layer of vegetables. Add salt and pepper. Cover salad bowl with plastic wrap and refrigerate.

Stick lettuce leaves around sides of bowl. When serving, dig through layers to give each guest a bit of each layer. The custom is to spoon Tabbouleh on a lettuce leaf and roll it up and eat it with your fingers.

Wild Rice Salad

To wash and make each wild rice kernel open "butterfly" fashion, see directions under recipe for Wild Rice with Almonds, page 7.

Remember never to cook wild rice in a pan over direct heat.

Wild rice is no relation to ordinary white rice. As an almost disappearing grass harvested primarily in Minnesota marshes, its price has skyrocketed because of its scarcity.

5 cups prepared wild rice (1½ cups raw)
1 leek, cleaned, thinly sliced
2 stalks celery, without leaves, finely chopped
1 carrot, finely chopped
⅓ green or red pepper, membrane and seeds removed, finely chopped
⅓ zucchini, finely chopped
½ cup parsley leaves, minced
2 Tablespoons olive oil
Salt and pepper, freshly ground, to taste

Serves 8-12

Put cooked "butterfly" wild rice into salad bowl. Add all remaining ingredients and toss well to mix thoroughly so each kernel of "butterfly" wild rice is coated with olive oil. Use your hands as well as salad spoon and fork to toss.

Cover salad bowl tightly with plastic wrap and leave in refrigerator at least four hours to meld. Serve cold. This salad needs no lettuce as an underpinning.

Honeyed Beer Bread

Everyone at your house will fight over this Honeyed Beer Bread. Served hot or cold, it's creature comforting and especially adaptable for a picnic or backyard frolic.

3 cups self-rising flour
1 Tablespoon honey,
** warmed**
One 12-oz. bottle or can of
** beer at room temperature**

One loaf pan, 9″ × 5″,
** oiled**

Makes one loaf
Preheat oven to 350°.
Pour flour in bowl. Add warmed honey and beer. Mix thoroughly until blended. Pour mixture into prepared pan. Bake 1½ hours.

Quick Herbed Onion Bread

This is a delicious, quick, easy bread to make, so you can enjoy the great luxury of having hot homemade bread with your dinner. The aroma of the herbs and the bread will act as a magnet to anyone in your home, as well as magnetizing the cook.

Quick Herbed Onion Bread is wonderful as long as it lasts: warm, cold or toasted.

½ cup milk
1½ Tablespoons sugar
1 teaspoon salt
1 Tablespoon butter
1 envelope (1 Tablespoon)
** yeast**
½ cup warm water
** (120°-130°)**
2¼ cups whole wheat flour
** or unbleached flour**
½ small onion, coarsely
** chopped**
½ teaspoon dill
1 teaspoon rosemary

One loaf pan, oiled

Makes one loaf
Preheat oven to 350°.
Scald milk and dissolve sugar, salt and butter in it. Cool to lukewarm. In a large bowl, dissolve yeast in warm water. Place dissolved yeast into food processor bowl fitted with steel blade. With motor running, pour cooled milk, flour, chopped onion and herbs through feed tube. Process briefly, but be careful not to overmix.

When batter is smooth, pour it into another bowl. Cover it with plastic wrap and let dough rise in a warm place until tripled in bulk (about 45 to 60 minutes). Turn it into prepared loaf pan. Place in oven at once to bake one hour.

Very Lemon Bread with Lemon Pour

Very Lemon Bread is accurately named and, when glazed with Lemon Pour, will delight all lemon fanciers. Very Lemon Bread, made a day ahead, is always an addition to a picnic basket or backyard party.

⅓ cup butter, melted
½ cup honey, warmed, or
  1 cup sugar
3 Tablespoons lemon extract
2 eggs
1½ cups flour
1 teaspoon baking powder
1 teaspoon salt
½ cup milk
1½ Tablespoons lemon zest
½ cup pecans, chopped
  (optional)

One 9″ × 5″ loaf pan,
  greased and floured

FOR THE LEMON POUR:
¼ cup lemon juice
Additional ½ cup honey,
  slightly warmed, or
  ½ cup sugar

TO ASSEMBLE:

Makes one loaf
Preheat oven to 350°.

In a large bowl, mix butter, honey or sugar, and lemon extract. Beat eggs into this butter mixture.

In another bowl, sift flour, baking powder and salt. Add flour mixture alternately with milk to the butter mixture. Beat just enough to blend. Fold in grated lemon zest and pecans, if desired. Pour batter into prepared loaf pan. Bake one hour or until an inserted toothpick comes out clean. Cool 10 minutes.

In small bowl, combine lemon juice with honey or sugar. Mix well.

While bread is still warm, remove from pan and drizzle Lemon Pour over top and into any cracks that formed while baking. Store, wrapped in foil, for one day before using.

5-3 Ice

When you are visiting former Denver residents who had the misfortune to be transferred elsewhere, this is a nifty recipe to take along. If you forget to bring it, you can simply remember it.

My changing the amount of the second item, (1¼ cups honey) admittedly, makes the recipe a bit more difficult to recall. The name of this recipe emanated from using five ingredients with three whatevers for each ingredient. But I reduced the caloric 3 cups sugar to 1¼ cups honey. This reduction works very nicely.

Anyway, do your best to remember it. If you think that is impossible, take the recipe along when you travel; then volunteer to make the dessert for the whole tribe you are visiting. Hope your hostess owns an ice cream freezer to alleviate your work. All of you will revel in this pure unadulterated flavor.

3 cups very hot water
1¼ cups honey
Juice of 3 oranges
Juice of 3 lemons
3 bananas, mashed

Makes 2 quarts

In a large bowl, mix hot water (just under the boiling point) with honey to melt. Stir in orange and lemon juices and mashed bananas. Mix thoroughly. Pour into bowl and place in deep freeze 30 minutes. Pour into ice cream freezer and freeze according to its directions.

Fresh Peach Ice Cream

Of all seasonal delights, Fresh Peach Ice Cream is the zenith. Don't even bother to make this recipe until you can buy ripe (not too ripe) rosy peaches at market, as canned peaches won't work.*

The creaminess, the sensational glimmer of fresh peaches and the texture of homemade ice cream combine to make this a dessert guests savor and remember all their lives. When you want to make a meal memorable, always serve Fresh Peach Ice Cream.

5 medium-size (about 5½ oz. each) ripe peaches make 1¼ cups peach purée
¼ cup honey
⅔ cup whipping cream
⅔ cup half-and-half
⅔ cup milk
1 teaspoon almond extract
1 teaspoon vanilla

Yield: 1½ qts.
(Serves 8-10)

Stone and peel peaches. Chop. Heat honey in an oiled glass measuring cup until just barely warm. If microwaving, heat at 50% power about 10 seconds, or place cup in pan with surrounding water and heat only until honey is barely warm.

In food processor bowl fitted with steel blade, place chopped peaches. Process to purée completely. Add barely warmed honey and process to mix. Let mixture rest ten minutes to meld. With motor running, through feed tube, pour whipping cream, half-and-half, milk, almond extract and vanilla. Process just to mix. Pour peach mixture into a separate bowl and place in freezer 30 minutes.

Into ice cream maker, pour peach mixture. Add salt and ice according to directions of ice cream maker. Plug in to make ice cream. The technique of placing peach mixture in freezer prior to placing in ice cream maker should halve your time for making ice cream. An energy-saving tip.

When ice cream maker rotates as if it is on its last gasp, the ice cream is ready. Spoon it into a bowl. Wrap tightly with plastic wrap. Place in freezer to ripen. Serve with chocolate cookies.

*Should you experience an uncontrollable urge for Peach Ice Cream in the dead of winter, use frozen peaches. Barely defrost them, and pour off excess liquid. Two 10-oz. packages of frozen peaches will yield the necessary 1¼ cups peach purée.

Green Tomato and Apple Pie
With Pastry Crusts

Formerly, green tomatoes were only available to gardeners and were especially profuse at the end of the growing season and tedious to use up, as no one has enough room to store the bushel baskets overflowing with them. But nowadays, green tomatoes are often lined up with other fresh fruits (tomatoes are not a vegetable, surprisingly) at your supermarket.

This recipe is the best rendition of apple pie I know. Furthermore, your guests will be completely baffled trying to guess what it is. No matter, because the combination of this incomparable crust with the tart green tomatoes and juicy apples is a sure fire hit any time.

FOR THE PASTRY CRUSTS:
3½ cups flour
10 oz. (20 Tablespoons) butter, chilled, cut into pieces
1 teaspoon sugar
½ teaspoon salt
1 egg yolk, beaten
⅓ to ½ cup iced water

One 10″ pie pan

FOR THE FILLING:
3 apples
3 green tomatoes
Juice of half lemon
½ cup brown sugar
Additional 1½ Tablespoons flour
Additional ½ teaspoon salt

Serves 8
For a 10″ pie pan
(top and bottom crusts)

In food processor bowl fitted with steel blade, place flour, butter, sugar and salt. Process quickly until mixture resembles coarse meal. With motor running, add beaten egg yolk through feed tube and process just until incorporated.

With motor still running, pour water slowly through feed tube until dough barely forms a ball. Remove dough to separate bowl.

Roll a little more than half the dough into a circle to make bottom crust. Circle must be at least 1½″ larger than diameter of the pie pan. Press it into pie pan. Refrigerate it and also refrigerate remaining dough, covered in plastic wrap.

Preheat oven to 375°.

Peel and core apples and tomatoes. In your food processor bowl fitted with thin-slicing disc (an extra attachment), push apples and tomatoes through feed tube. With medium pressure, process to slice.

You don't yet have a food processor? Use your trusty knife, and your slices may even look prettier.

Place sliced apples and green tomatoes in a bowl and immediately sprinkle lemon juice over them to preserve color. Add sugar, flour and salt and stir to mix thoroughly. Spoon the filling into the uncooked pie shell.

Roll out remaining dough and make an additional circle to cover the pie. Place it on top of pie. With a wet thumb and forefinger, crimp the edges of the two crusts together to seal tightly. With a sharp knife, slash the top crust 4 to 5 times to allow steam to escape. Bake pie on bottom rack of oven about 45 minutes. Serve pie warm or cool.

Picnics and Backyard Frolics
(Alias Barbecues)

Orange Poppy Seed Cake

Orange Poppy Seed Cake is a tasty, healthful combination of flavors. It is the very thing to take in your picnic basket or to serve at a backyard frolic.

4 oz. unsalted butter,
  softened
½ cup honey, warmed, or
  ¾ cup sugar
2 eggs
½ cup plain yogurt
⅓ cup poppy seeds
  (reserve 1 Tablespoon)
¼ cup fresh orange juice
1 Tablespoon orange zest,
  grated
1 teaspoon vanilla
1¼ cups unbleached flour
½ teaspoon double-acting
  baking powder
¼ teaspoon baking soda
⅛ teaspoon salt

GARNISH:
Powdered sugar
Reserved 1 Tablespoon
  poppy seeds

One 1-qt. decorative cake mold,
  buttered and floured

Serves 12-16

Preheat oven to 350°.

Into food processor bowl fitted with steel blade, process to combine softened butter and honey or sugar. With food processor's motor running, drop eggs, one at a time, through feed tube.

In another bowl with rubber spatula, mix yogurt, poppy seeds, orange juice, grated orange zest and vanilla. Set aside.

Sift together flour, baking powder, baking soda and salt. Add flour mixture to butter-egg mixture in food processor bowl. Process briefly until mixtures are integrated. Remove and add to orange-yogurt mixture in bowl. Mix thoroughly.

Pour batter into prepared mold. Bake in oven 45 to 55 minutes (baking time will depend on shape of your mold), or until an inserted straw comes out clean. Remove baked cake from oven and let cake rest ten minutes before inverting onto cake rack. Dust top with powdered sugar and reserved 1 Tablespoon poppy seeds.

Pineapple-on-a-Spit

For an extra fancy presentation, serve pineapple treated this way with a luscious strawberry or raspberry purée. But never fear: Pineapple-on-a-Spit can stand alone for it is unique. Even if you skip the sugar, this is a light, wholesome, yet party-time dessert.

One medium-ripe pineapple
2-3 Tablespoons sugar
  (optional)
6 Tablespoons Cointreau
  (orange liqueur)

Serves 6

Peel pineapple. Discard top frond, but leave pineapple whole. Do not core. Place it in a large bowl. With pastry brush, baste pineapple in mixture of sugar and Cointreau. Marinate several hours, as you baste often. Reserve marinade.

About one hour before serving, with pineapple-corer, zucchini knife or paring knife, core pineapple. Put skewer with one fastener through hole of pineapple and add other fastener. Attach and tighten both fasteners. Maintain broiler at low temperature and rotate skewer slowly. It is necessary to baste with reserved marinade every 15 minutes. Marinade will carmelize on pineapple.

If you don't have a rôtisserie, put large pan with pineapple under broiler at low temperature, as far away from broiler as oven will allow. Hover over it. You must baste every 10 minutes as you turn pineapple. Watch carefully so marinade will not burn. Slice pineapple into sixths and serve hot.

Plugged Melon

This recipe is a godsend, particularly when melons are at their prime at market. You can plug a melon in about 30 seconds (time yourself), yet your guests will be so fascinated with this presentation, they will never dream that it is such a quickie to execute.

Besides, the combination of wine with melon produces a happy marriage, with the offspring being that melon never tasted so refreshing.

This recipe is a sterling example of a very simple recipe that reaches gastronomic heights, especially when it is eaten outdoors.

One ripe melon (Persian, casaba, honeydew or your choice)
½-1 cup table red, white or rosé wine of your choice

Number of servings depends on size of melon

With a sharp pointed knife, make a triangle 1¼"-1½" (actual size depends on size of melon) in side of melon. Cut through flesh to extricate entire triangle. With an iced-teaspoon or small small spoon with a long handle, remove all seeds from melon. Pour wine in cavity. Replug triangle. Refrigerate at least four hours before serving.

To serve, pour wine from melon into bowl. Slice melon. On each individual plate, place a slice of melon and pour wine over it.

Brandy Snaps

Brandy Snaps are one of the truly chic cookies of all time. They are a bit tricky to execute but, once you know how, couldn't be simpler.

Originally from England, this recipe from one of the top British cooks, Marika, uses golden syrup with powdered ginger. The combination produces an unforgettable flavor. Brandy Snaps are somewhat fragile. They should be placed in a tin for easy transporting.

Brandy Snaps are the crowning touch to an outdoor feast or to any dinner party anywhere.

2 Tablespoons golden syrup*
⅓ cup superfine sugar
2 oz. butter
2 oz. cake flour
1 teaspoon powdered ginger
1 teaspoon brandy

One cookie sheet, ungreased

***Golden syrup, emanating from England, comes in various size bottles, and will be found in gourmet sections of markets. If not there, ask for it, as it imparts a special flavor.**

Makes 10-12

Preheat oven to 300°.

In pan over medium heat, pour golden syrup, sugar and butter. Cook until sugar is dissolved. Let cool slightly.

In food processor bowl fitted with steel blade, add flour and ginger and process briefly to mix. With motor running, through feed tube, pour cooled syrup. Process just enough to incorporate. Add brandy. Process briefly to mix.

Drop Brandy Snaps by about one teaspoonful each onto cookie sheet. Bake 10 to 12 minutes on rack in middle of oven. Bake until Brandy Snaps become light brown.

To roll Brandy Snaps to resemble lilies: do not attempt to roll until they are slightly cooled. If they are rolled when very hot, cookies will collapse.

Turn over each cookie before rolling to present the better looking side. Roll each cookie like a cornucopia around the handle of a wooden spoon. Remove to platter. Keep cookie sheet warm while rolling other cookies. If necessary, return cookie sheet to oven to keep warm.

Brandy Snaps may be filled with pastry cream or ice cream, if you wish, and will make a complete dessert.

FOR PRESENTATION:
For eye-catching appeal, arrange Brandy Snaps like spokes in a wheel on a round platter or plate.

Pecan Moons

Nifty to take on a picnic or to serve at home, as their chewy texture coupled with their nutty flavor make the cook want to eat the whole batch. Once you've tasted one, you simply haven't the will power to stop.

1¼ cups pecans
1 cup light brown sugar
2 egg whites

One cookie sheet, buttered

Makes about 60

Preheat oven to 325°.

Into food processor bowl fitted with steel blade, place pecans. Process until they resemble fine bread crumbs, but do not overprocess lest they become a mass. Remove to medium-size bowl.

Put sugar into food processor bowl, still fitted with steel blade, and process to remove any lumps.

Beat egg whites until stiff and glossy. Add brown sugar gradually as you continue to beat. Fold in finely chopped pecans. Drop by about ¾ teaspoonful onto prepared cookie sheet. Bake about 12 minutes. Pecan moons should be barely brown.

With a metal spatula, remove Pecan Moons from cookie sheet to a plate or platter (do not put on top of each other) while they are still warm. They will crisp as they cool.

Tried-and-True
Chocolate Chip Cookies

A trendy New York store sells a chocolate chip cookie mix. In Denver, many cooks prefer to make their own from scratch. So easy, too. With the food processor, you will be glad you gave this recipe a try.

Ever since this recipe was developed 45 years ago at the Toll House Restaurant, Chocolate Chip Cookies have been a part of the American food culture. So much so, that there is an ever-growing cult of chocolate chip cookie fans. The cookies ar perfect for a picnic or a backyard spree, as they can be made ahead. But, remember to hide them, as family have been known to sneakily devour them, leaving the cook with an empty cookie jar.

The original recipe, called "Toll House Chocolate Crunch Cookies" calls for Nestle's 7-oz. yellow label chocolate, semi-sweet, cut in pieces the size of a pea. (Cooks today only open a package of semi-sweet chocolate morsels.)

In a revival of the **Toll House Tried and True Recipes** cookbook, there is advice to chill the dough, with this pearl about the cookies: *"They should be brown through, and crispy, not white and hard as I have sometimes seen them."* So don't be guilty.

**4 oz. unsalted butter,
cut up, chilled**
½ cup brown sugar
**2 Tablespoons honey, warmed,
or ½ cup granulated sugar**
1 egg
**1 cup and 1 additional
Tablespoon unbleached flour**
½ teaspoon salt
**½ teaspoon baking soda,
mixed in small cup
with ½ teaspoon hot water**
**1 package (12-oz.) semi-sweet
chocolate morsels**
½ teaspoon vanilla
**½ cup pecans, chopped
(optional)**

One cookie sheet, buttered

Makes about 30 cookies
Preheat oven to 375°.

Into food processor bowl fitted with steel blade, place chilled butter around blades. Add brown sugar with honey or granulated sugar. Process to mix. With motor running, add egg through feed tube. Process briefly.

Sift flour and salt together. With food processor's motor running, add flour mixture to mixture in bowl alternately with dissolved baking soda. Process just long enough to mix. Remove mixture to another bowl. Add chocolate morsels and vanilla. Add pecans, if desired. Wrap dough in plastic wrap and refrigerate at least 2 hours.

Drop by half-teaspoonsful on cookie sheet, or roll with your hands. Flatten each cookie with thumb and forefinger. Bake on top rack about 8 minutes to achieve perfect degree of crispness, but watch carefully after first six minutes of baking time. Remove from cookie sheet at once, while cookies are still warm. Lay cookies flat on platter or plates to cool. .

Crêpes

Chapter V

Exploding the Mystique of Crêpes

Serving crêpes is not only chic, but relatively inexpensive. They are easy to accomplish once you know how to make them. Do use some original ideas (or steal recipes) on what filling to choose.

A crêpe is a pancake with charisma. Its versatility is apparent as it can cuddle cubed chicken, an assortment of sea food, a vegetable medley, or ice cream or fruit. And a crêpe is the best disguise ever for leftover food.

Furthermore, it may be served as an appetizer, a luncheon dish or, of course, a dessert. This choice morsel also may be served alone, folded into a triangle, bathed in liqueurs or fruit juices, and the ultimate—flamed in brandy. Crêpes may even be piled one on top of the other with an appropriate filling and made into a cake.

Not to worry how to pronounce crêpes. You either may say "kreps" to rhyme with "steps" or "krapes" to rhyme with "grapes". Spell it with or without the French hat accent circumflex - over the first "e".

Sometimes one feels that crêperies are enfolding the entire country with crêpes, since the entire menu consists of crêpes. So why are crêpes so universally popular today?

Crêpes have some assets that are hard to beat. First and foremost is the fact that they can be made ahead, stacked, layered between sheets of waxed paper, and either frozen or refrigerated. So all the cook has to cope with on the day they are to be served is making the filling, spooning it inside the crêpes and shaping them. At the last minute, reheat and, if you wish, flame them. Although these are several steps, happily, they can be executed in lightning time.

Crêpes are so tender they can easily be cut with a fork. Be very sure that everything in the filling is bite-size so no knife is necessary to cut anything. Paradoxically, a crêpe is still so hardy it can be folded into any shape without its breaking or tearing. It is sturdy enough to enfold compactly and firmly any filling you, as cook, could conceive—and that is enough to recommend crêpes to anyone.

Equipment for Crêpes

A few years back, there was a rash of upside-down crêpe pans for sale at kitchen equipment stores. A few of these crêpe pans are still around. Each crêpe is cooked on the bottom of the pan, either over gas or electric heat, or some upside-down crêpe pans are completely electric. The bottom of the pan (turned into the top) has to have a very thin coating of batter for cooking the crêpe. The problem is that it is difficult, if not impossible, to dip the bottom of the pan properly into the batter so that it spreads thinly and evenly.

If you do opt for using this type of crêpe pan, quickly buy yourself a saucer about 3 inches larger in diameter than your crêpe pan. But take my word for it, when you get to the dregs of the batter, you may lose your good disposition as you dip.

Before you invest in a certain medium-priced all-electric crêpe maker, look at the unit underneath the pan with a jaundiced eye. I discovered that it was an almighty pain to keep clean; but if that fact does not worry you, it is advertised to make foolproof crêpes.

So much easier, I think, to buy and use an old-fashioned crêpe pan, virtually a small skillet. Crêpes are usually 5 inches in diameter, but some crêpes, especially for entrées, are often as large as 6 inches in diameter.

When purchasing a crêpe pan, do try to find one with a non-stick coating. This will cut calories, as you will need to use less butter or oil in which to cook the crêpes.

Also, for broiling or oven-warming filled and sauced crêpes, try to find a shallow broiling pan with a non-stick surface. This will eliminate the need for oiling pans.

Seasoning of New Crêpe Pan

Whatever you buy, a new crêpe pan needs to be seasoned. Coat it with a tasteless safflower or vegetable oil (nothing strong like olive oil). Then heat pan until it is very, very hot. Most crêpe devotees use this pan solely for making crêpes, but that all depends on how many pots and pans you may own. But do remember never to wash your crêpe pan with soap and water. Simply wipe it out with more oil and paper towels.

Making Crêpe Batter

Let your imagination soar as you concoct a filling for your crêpes, but follow directions to the letter when preparing the batter from scratch for crêpes. It is particularly important to measure flour correctly. Using a one-third cup dry measure, dip it into the flour sack or bin and fill measure. Using the back of a knife, level measure. Carefully measure flour in this manner three times. Of course, then you have a perfect full cup of flour.

Another way to measure flour correctly is to weigh it on kitchen scales. When you are measuring ingredients for the crêpe batter, do it scientifically, as the recipe specifies, rather than "by guess and by golly".

Also, when making crêpe batter, be wary of overbeating. If using food processor, don't overprocess, as tough batter will only produce tough pancakes.

Cooking a Crêpe

After your crêpe batter has rested, refrigerated, its appropriate time per directions for individual recipes, it is ready for cooking. The crêpe pan must be heated until it is very hot. Try the trick of putting a blob of water on it. When the water dances, your pan is hot enough and all set to cook crêpes.

Perfect crêpes must be parchment thin—no more than one-sixteenth inch thick. If you want a 5-inch-in-diameter crêpe, the average size, the easiest way is to use a jigger with a pouring lip. Fill jigger just under ounce mark or with 1½ tablespoons batter. If you want a six-inch-in-diameter crêpe and if you are using a jigger, use just barely over an ounce or 2 tablespoons batter. Naturally, you may use a spoon or ladle in place of the jigger if you wish.

When you intend to use an upside-down crêpe pan, find a deep enough receptacle in which to house and dip the batter. A pie pan, or any pan with sides will not work, as usually the long wooden handle of the crêpe pan hits against it. So if you can find a special deep ceramic pan, about 8½ inches in diameter, it will work wonders. Dip your hot crêpe pan into batter and then count to four. Quickly remove it from batter before cooking starts, and place crêpe pan over heat.

Turn the heat under your crêpe pan to medium, not high heat. If any holes appear in crêpe while it is cooking, the trick is simply to spoon a small amount of batter into any hole to fill in. So easy once you know how.

When the crêpe you are cooking begins to look dry, and is bubbling from the center and browning slightly around the edges, loosen edges with a spatula. Flip crêpe over. If you can't manage this feat yourself yet, magically conjure up the perennial chef on television flipping a crêpe. You must have seen that operation a million times. Just copy him in your kitchen when no one is looking. It's fun and easy and makes you feel as if you are a real pro. With practice, you'll get the timing. But flipping never guarantees a well cooked, fragile pancake.

Just like the cooks who make them, each crêpe has an inside and an outside. The bottom side which cooks first, always browns more evenly than the side cooked last. The latter is invariably spotty.

Cooking a crêpe is quick and easy. There is no better way for you to learn how to manage the making and cooking of crêpes than for you just to dive in, and practice a couple of rounds on the family before you make them for company.

Very often the first crêpe you cook will have to be discarded, then the crêpe pan settles down to honest-and-true crêpe making. Don't worry about tossing away such a small scrap. Consider it the test case.

The perfect crêpe should be blonde, barely browned and not crusty. This is easier when there is no sweetening in the batter, because both sugar and honey have a tendency to brown too quickly, even burn! It is a great temptation when cooking crêpes to let them just lie there and cook away. But if you do that, your crêpes will not be pliable nor will they roll, nor fold, nor shape up in the manner you choose. So don't leave a crêpe while it is cooking to answer the telephone or to work on another dish on your menu. A crêpe is cooked in seconds.

Storing of Crêpes

Prepare several squares of waxed paper to put between your crêpes. The size of the square must be slightly larger than the size of the crêpes you are cooking. The second side of each crêpe will cook faster than the first. It will cook in just about a minute, from the time you turn over the pancake. Remove crêpe from pan to platter or plate and cover with a square of waxed paper. Continue layering crêpes between waxed paper squares until all batter is used.

Feel free to deep freeze this stack of crêpes, or place stack in refrigerator. Your choice depends on when you plan to use them. If you never want to be caught in a crunch, always have a stacked pile of crêpes in your freezer, ready for unexpected company.

Filling of Crêpes

A crêpe itself is not a fantastic taste treat (unless it has a smidge of liqueur in its batter). A crêpe is merely a vehicle to carry a filling. Yet, it's an inspired and economical way to use up leftovers hanging around your refrigerator.

Just as with soufflés, crêpes may be divided into savory crêpes and dessert crêpes. The main difference is that the batter of the former is made without any sweetening or any liqueur. Savory crêpes, however, may be used in a pinch in lieu of dessert crêpes, but never vice versa.

After you make fillings for crêpes a few times, you can really go hog wild, not needing a written recipe at all. Use whatever you have around, fresh or leftover. Then create a sauce to bind it together and hold the filling within the crêpe. Season the filling as imaginatively as you can. Whee! You have then concocted a wonderful new filling recipe. My recipes for fillings that follow are the ones which have been the most popular at our house over the years.

To Shape a Crêpe

So at this point, the crêpes are well-stacked in the freezer or refrigerator. No matter where they were stored, they must be brought to room temperature so that they will fold properly. While this is occurring, make your filling and have it ready.

You will have to choose among several ways to fold and present your crêpes. The most popular crêpe shape is the Fold-Over. This is evident in almost every restaurant scene where that is the typical crêpe presentation. A Fold-Over is easy to effect, with its filling peeking out both ends, so the diner knows exactly what he is eating. Place the better-looking side of your crêpe down flat on the kitchen counter and spoon the filling along center of crêpe. Fold one side over, covering most of the filling. Then fold over the opposite side. Overlap your first fold a bit, and you have it. The finished Fold-Over resembles a cigar roll but, fortunately, is prettier.

Another alternative is to make the Half-Fold when shaping a crêpe. This is particularly appropriate when you have a large, gooey filling. Again, place the better looking side of the crêpe down flat. Spoon filling horizontally to cover half of inside of crêpe. Simply fold crêpe to make a half-moon. Such an easy way to shape crêpes.

Still another shape is the Roll-Up. Spread filling over entire crêpe (this works wonderfully with either jam or jelly). You guessed it: roll it up like a jelly roll.

The Burrito Roll is handy for any crêpe filling which might become runny when heated. Spread filling over inside of crêpe (outer side of crêpe is always the better side), but leave about a one-half inch border around edge of crêpe. Or, spoon filling into center of crêpe.

First fold right side in, and then fold left side in, to cover filling. Start at the bottom of the crêpe and roll up. Make sure that the sides are folded in as you roll up.

The Blintz is also known as the Pocket-Fold Roll. Spoon filling into center of pancake. Fold bottom of crêpe over almost half the filling. Fold right side of crêpe a bit more than half over the filling. Repeat with left side of crêpe as you overlap the right side. Next fold crêpe down almost to center where both sides overlap. Some gentlemen fold their pocket handkerchiefs in this fashion. It does produce a neat little package.

Of all folds, the two easiest are the Crêpe Suzette Fold and assembling crêpes to make a "Cake". For a Crêpe Suzette Fold, spoon filling in center of crêpe and fold in half. Fold crêpe in half again, forming a triangle four layers thick. Get it?

Here's the easiest of all: assembling "crêpes" to make the "Cake" or "Gâteau". Simply stack one crêpe on top of another. Sandwich in-between with whatever is your heart's desire, be it ice cream, a pastry cream, fruit or whipped cream, or a mixture of any of these. The only advice is to have a filling that is firm enough not to run.

If you want to be extra fancy and throw all caution to the winds, cover entire "cake" or "gâteau" with whipped cream and decorate with fresh fruit.

A Crêpe Party

If you have been wanting to host a party to upstage your cook-friend rival, a crêpe party will be extravagantly admired not only by your cook-friend, but by all your other guests as well. It is actually a very simple, inexpensive party to host, as all you need to provide is an unending stack of crêpes with bowls of prospective fillings. Decide on savory or dessert crêpes, or have both.

Have bowls full of varied fillings on a table, where a guest can help himself. One bowl might have a meat filling, another could contain seafood, and still another, a vegetable medley. Also, serve separate bowls with stunning garnishes. Depending on how many guests you invite, have a bowl or two with sauces. Let each guest fill his own crêpe and then sauce it with his preference. Then, either the host or the guest can return the filled crêpe briefly to the oven to reheat it quickly under a medium broiler.

If your guest list consists of a cast of dozens, obviously, you must simplify such a production and settle solely on a dessert crêpe party. This is much easier because nothing has to be reheated. (Of course, omit Crêpes Suzette or other crêpes needing flaming.)

For dessert crêpes, have bowls of fresh fruit, bowls of jellies and jams, bowls of various kinds of fruit ices and ice creams. And don't forget the whipped cream. Let each guest choose his own filling, and then shape his crêpes as he sees fit. See who is the artist in the crowd.

When you give a crêpe party, you will be proclaimed the host or hostess of the year. Best of all, you really did not have to work terribly hard to pull the party off triumphantly.

Don't forget that when you serve crêpes at your house, any meal is transformed into a party. That is the mystique of crêpes.

All-Purpose Crêpe Batter

This is a very rich batter which works equally well for savory or dessert crêpes. A stack of these crêpes in your freezer will be most handy when unexpected company comes knocking at your door.

Although only the food processor method is spelled out in my recipe, feel free to use a blender or a whisk and your results will be every bit as good.

4 oz. unsalted
butter, melted
4 eggs
⅛ teaspoon salt
2 cups flour
1 cup milk
¾ cup half-and-half
¼ cup water

Serves 8-10
Makes twenty-four 5″ crepes

To melt butter in microwave, place butter in glass measuring cup. Microwave 20 seconds at 50% power. See if additional microwave time is required. Remember to turn cup. When butter is melted, remove cup from oven.

In food processor bowl fitted with plastic blade, add eggs with salt. Process briefly to mix. With motor running, alternately pour, through feed tube, flour and liquid mixture of milk, half-and-half and water. Process until batter is well mixed and free from lumps. With motor running, pour melted butter gradually through feed tube. Process until integrated. Refrigerate batter at least one hour, and preferably two hours, before cooking. Make crêpes, following my guidelines in "Exploding the Mystique of Crêpes".

Classic Dessert Crêpe Batter

Down through the annals of crêpe cooking techniques comes this classic recipe for crêpe batter. Making crêpes is an absolute cinch in a food processor, but remember to let the batter rest, refrigerated.

When not serving crêpes as dessert, simply omit sugar and vanilla from this recipe and you have a notable recipe for savory crêpe batter. Incidentally, in a pinch, savory crêpes may be used in lieu of dessert crêpes.

1 cup unbleached flour
3 eggs
1 Tablespoon superfine sugar
¼ teaspoon salt
1½ cups milk
1 teaspoon vanilla

FOR COOKING CRÊPES:
 3 Tablespoons unsalted
 butter, melted (may be
 omitted when using a
 non-stick pan)

Serves 6-8
Makes fifteen to eighteen
 5″ crêpes

How you measure the flour in this recipe is of the utmost importance. Use a ⅓ cup dry measure. Dip it into flour canister or bag and level with a knife. Repeat two additional times.

In food processor bowl fitted with plastic blade, pour flour. With motor running, add eggs, one at a time, through feed tube, with sugar and salt. Pour milk gradually and process until well mixed and batter is free from lumps. Add vanilla and process briefly. Pour batter into separate bowl and refrigerate.

Batter should rest at least one-half hour, but preferably two hours, in order that flour can absorb liquid. Then, the batter will produce a more fragile pancake.

To cook crêpes, with a pastry brush, first coat bottom and sides of crêpe pan with melted butter. Heat pan over medium-high heat. Then, pour just enough crêpe batter (2 to 3 Tablespoons) into crêpe pan to cover bottom of pan. If your crêpe pan has a non-stick coating, omit coating with butter.

Tilt pan to swirl the batter so that it completely covers the bottom of pan in a very thin layer. Cook crêpe until bottom is brown. Using a metal spatula, gently reverse pancake. Brown other side briefly. Remove from pan. Stack crêpes on platter or plate and cover each pancake with waxed paper.

My Favorite Basic Crêpe Batter

Of all recipes for crêpe batters, this is my favorite because it is quick, easy and adaptable. Besides, it is low-cholesterol, yet produces a very thin, fragile pancake. Should you be making savory crêpes, you may substitute beer for the 2 cups water, or use half beer and half water.

For dessert crêpes, add to this basic batter recipe, 1 Tablespoon honey, warmed, or 2 Tablespoons superfine sugar and 1 Tablespoon vanilla. For variation, add 2 Tablespoons brandy in place of vanilla.

For a really classy treatment, pour the same liqueur you are using in the filling into the batter, too. For instance, if your filling has Grand Marnier liqueur in it, pour 2 Tablespoons Grand Marnier in the actual crêpe batter.

2 eggs
2 cups quick mixing instant
　flour
2 cups water

Makes twenty-five 5″ crêpes

In food processor bowl fitted with plastic blade, place eggs and process to mix. With motor running, alternately pour flour and water through feed tube. Process to mix thoroughly.

Because of using quick mixing instant flour, this batter needs to rest only 20 minutes at room temperature prior to making crêpes. Follow directions under recipe for "Classic Dessert Crêpe Batter" for making individual crêpes.

Beer Crêpe Batter

This is a pertinent example of adding to your crêpe batter a certain ingredient which has an affinity with the filling you are creating. By themselves, crêpes taste very bland, but when you add beer, for instance, they immediately take on a certain pizzazz. Need I remind you that beer has an affinity with meat and seafood fillings?

2 eggs
Additional 1 egg yolk
1 cup quick mixing instant
　flour
1 teaspoon salt
1 cup beer
1 Tablespoon yogurt
1 Tablespoon melted butter

Serves 8
Makes eighteen to
**　twenty 5″ crêpes**

Into food processor bowl fitted with plastic blade, place eggs and additional egg yolk and process to mix. With motor running, alternately pour flour with salt and beer. Process to mix batter so that there are no lumps.

Remove batter to separate bowl. Add yogurt. Mix. Add melted butter and stir to mix. Since you are using quick mixing instant flour, batter needs to rest only 20 to 30 minutes at room temperature.

Follow directions under recipe for "Classic Dessert Crêpe Batter" to make individual crêpes. Remember in order to make one crêpe, pour small amount of batter (usually only 2 Tablespoons) to coat the bottom of pan as thinly as possible.

97

Beer Crêpes Filled with Seafood

In any French kitchen alphabet, "c" is for crêpes. We should adopt this French custom. No better place to start than with this seafood crêpe entrée. I have never tasted a better crêpe filling.

Because of the exorbitant price of certain fish, the original recipe, specifying expensive shrimp and crabmeat, has been skimmed down. I am substituting turbot and using as few shrimp as possible. You will find my fish combination exciting as well as more economical.

3 oz. butter
⅓ cup flour
1½ bunches scallions with tops,
  chopped
1-2 cloves garlic, minced
2 Tablespoons tomato paste
  or purée
2-3 teaspoons curry powder
1 teaspoon salt
1 teaspoon white pepper
1 cup clam juice
  (from 7-oz. bottle)
  or homemade fish stock
1¼ cups cream
1½ lbs. medium-size uncooked
  shrimp (weigh without
  shells)
1½ lbs. turbot or sole
¼ cup fresh lemon juice
2 cups mushrooms, sliced
⅓ cup parsley, minced
3-4 drops Tabasco
16 beer crêpes
  at room temperature
  (see recipe for "Beer Crêpe
  Batter")

FOR THE TOPPING:
2-3 Tablespoons grated
  Parmesan cheese

One broiler pan or shallow
  rectangular pan, lightly
  oiled.

Serves 8
Two filled crêpes for
  each serving

Into a large skillet, place 2 oz. of the butter to melt. Whisk in flour. Cook 2 to 3 minutes. Add scallions and garlic. Cook about 3 minutes until soft. Stir in tomato paste. Cook an additional 5 minutes. Add seasonings. Add clam juice and cream. Mix thoroughly. Bring mixture to a boil. Add shrimp and turbot, both cut into bite-size pieces. Reduce heat to cook fish mixture slowly until shrimp turn pink (about 5 minutes). Remove pan from heat but keep mixture warm.

In a separate large skillet, melt remaining 1 oz. butter. Stir in 1 teaspoon of the lemon juice with mushrooms. Sauté them until liquid has evaporated (about 7 minutes). Add mushroom mixture to fish mixture with remaining lemon juice, parsley and Tabasco. Stir until well mixed.

Preheat broiler to medium.

Lay crêpe with browner side down on working surface. Spoon about 1½-2 Tablespoons seafood filling into center of each crêpe and roll up to enfold filling. Fill all crêpes.

Place filled crêpes close to each other in shallow pan. Top with grated cheese. Place under broiler for about 6 to 10 minutes, until crêpes are bubbly and hot. Serve at once.

Scallops and Leek Crêpes

This is another example of an inimitable filling for crêpes. Scallops and Leek filling can be whipped up in jiffy time, spooned inside each crêpe, and then reheated just before serving.

2 leeks
6 Tablespoons butter
6 Tablespoons flour
2 cups milk
¾ cup chicken stock
1 oz. dry sherry
1½ lbs. bay scallops*
  (about 80 to a lb.)
Salt and pepper, freshly
  ground, to taste
½ teaspoon nutmeg, grated

16 cooked savory crêpes

Broiler pan or shallow
  rectangular pan
  lightly oiled

*If bay scallops are unavailable, buy sea scallops and cut into bite-size pieces.

Serves 8

Clean leeks carefully to see that all that pesky sand is removed. Slice thinly. Melt butter in skillet over high heat. Sauté leeks until soft. Lower heat to medium and whisk in flour. Gradually pour in milk and chicken stock, as you continue to whisk. When sauce is smooth and thick, pour in sherry. Continue to whisk.

Just before serving (5 to 10 minutes), add scallops. They should be warmed and barely cooked. Season with salt and pepper. Grate nutmeg over top.

Preheat broiler to medium.

Spoon about 1-1½ Tablespoons scallop mixture into center of each crêpe. Fold both sides of crêpe over to enclose scallop mixture. Lay crêpes flat in shallow pan. Place pan under broiler about 6 to 10 minutes. Watch carefully. Crêpes should be tinged with brown, but not browned. Mixture should be bubbly. Serve hot.

Crêpes

Spinach and Chicken Crêpes
with Sherried Cheese Sauce

Looking for an entrée filling for your well-stacked crêpes in your freezer? Look no more. Here is a filler that is also a thriller, more particularly when you make the recipe with fresh spinach. Using a fresh vegetable with a leftover anything gives the recipe a fresh and renewed taste.

This entrée would be supreme for an early or late supper, following some event, or racy for any luncheon you are hosting any time of the year. The accompanying Sherried Cheese Sauce is what makes the dish a thriller.

FOR THE FILLING:
2 oz. butter
½ lb. mushrooms, finely chopped
2 bunches scallions with tops, finely chopped
2 shallots, finely chopped
1 lb. fresh spinach, washed, stems removed, chopped (one 10-oz. package frozen spinach with liquid removed may be substituted)
3 cups cooked chicken, diced
¼ cup plain yogurt
¼ cup dry sherry
⅛ teaspoon cayenne
¼ teaspoon salt

FOR THE SHERRIED CHEESE SAUCE:
Additional 2 oz. butter
¼ cup flour
1 cup milk
2 cups chicken stock
1 cup Parmesan or Swiss cheese, shredded
Additional ½ cup dry sherry
Additional ⅛ teaspoon cayenne

TO ASSEMBLE:
16-20 cooked savory crêpes
One shallow broiler pan, buttered

To fill sixteen to twenty sugarless crêpes

In a large skillet or sauté pan, melt butter. Sauté mushrooms, scallions and shallots until soft. If mixture becomes too watery, boil down until most of the liquid evaporates. Stir in chopped spinach and chicken. Remove pan from heat. Stir in yogurt, sherry and seasonings.

In medium-size skillet or pan, melt butter. Whisk in flour to make roux. See that this mixture is free from lumps, and let flour cook about 2 minutes before adding milk and chicken stock gradually. Stir in cheese and let it melt completely. When mixture is smooth, add sherry and cayenne. Keep sauce warm or reheat until warm.

Preheat broiler to medium heat.
Be sure crêpes are at room temperature so they will be pliable. Lay the better side of the crêpe outside, flat on your working surface. Spoon in approximately 1½ Tablespoons spinach and chicken filling into center of crêpe and roll up crêpe. Lay crêpes flat side-by-side in broiler pan. Cover with Sherried Cheese Sauce. Place pan under medium broiler about 6 to 10 minutes until mixture is hot and bubbly. Serve hot at once. Usually serve two to each customer.

Vegetable Crêpes

Vegetable Crêpes are hearty enough to be served with only a salad as accompaniment. They would also be memorable served with fish or poultry to create a more robust meal. The crunchiness of the vegetables emerging from the delicacy of the crêpe results in a neat combination.

FOR THE BATTER:
⅔ cup milk
⅔ cup flour
4 eggs
2 Tablespoons butter, melted
⅛ teaspoon salt

FOR THE VEGETABLES:
2 medium-size leeks, cleaned, coarsely chopped
4 cloves garlic, chopped
2 medium-size green peppers, membrane and seeds removed, coarsely chopped
2 medium-size zucchini
6 Tablespoons olive oil
¼ lb. (about 1⅔ cups) mushrooms, cleaned
2 large tomatoes, seeded, quartered
2 teaspoons basil
4 teaspoons parsley leaves, chopped
Salt and pepper, freshly ground, to taste

Serves 8
Makes sixteen crêpes

Into food processor bowl fitted with plastic blade, place all ingredients and process one minute. Batter should be free of lumps. Pour batter into separate bowl to refrigerate for 30 minutes.

In food processor fitted with steel blade, place chopped leeks and garlic around blades. Process to chop finely. Remove to separate bowl.

Add chopped green pepper around steel blade of food processor and process to chop finely. Add to leeks in separate bowl.

Change to grater of food processor and cut zucchini to fit feed tube. With motor running, push zucchini through feed tube to grate.

Heat olive oil in skillet over high heat. When sizzling, add leeks with garlic and green pepper and sauté until leeks are transparent. Lower heat.

Change to steel blade of food processor and add mushrooms. Process quickly to chop fine, but not pureé. Put zucchini and mushrooms in separate bowl. Add quartered tomatoes to food processor bowl and process briefly to chop to bite-size, but be wary of overprocessing. Use on-off pulse. Do not leave motor running.

Add zucchini, mushrooms and tomatoes to leek mixture, cooking over medium heat. Add basil, parsley, salt and pepper. Sauté mixture until excess moisture disappears. Remove pan from heat. Let cool. Add batter mixture to vegetables.

(continued on next page)

TO ASSEMBLE:
3 Tablespoons unsalted butter

**2 cookie sheets, lightly
  oiled**

Preheat broiler to medium heat.

Melt butter in heavy skillet. You can make two crêpes at a time in one pan, or if you are adept, have two skillets heating simultaneously, so you can hasten the crêpe making process. Use about ½ teaspoon melted butter in which to cook each crêpe. Fry until golden. Turn over and fry. Place on cookie sheets. Run quickly under broiler to warm just before serving.

Crêpes Suzette

Is there any dessert more famous than Crêpes Suzette? Long ago and far away, an apprentice chef made a "horrific accident" in front of, of all people, Edward, Prince of Wales, the son of Queen Victoria. The chef unintentionally flamed the brandy. He coped extraordinarily well and just happened to concoct a dessert that is now a legend.

Prince Edward wanted the dish named for a little girl in their party named Suzette, but you may change the name to your own, when you produce such a chef d'oeuvre at table. Once you learn how, flame the crêpes at table. The simple trick is to warm the brandy first.

Consuming the exquisitely delicious melody of flavors in Crêpes Suzette easily could be the impetus for a switch from a cannibal to a civilized lady or gentleman.

The happiest part of this recipe is that the sauce can be made ahead and stored in a jar. Refrigerated, it will last indefinitely.

FOR THE SAUCE:
⅓-½ cup unsalted butter
½ cup fresh orange juice
2 teaspoons fresh lemon juice
½ cup Cointreau (orange liqueur)
½ cup Grand Marnier liqueur
½ cup and additional
  1 Tablespoon honey or
  ⅓ cup superfine sugar
2 teaspoons grated orange zest

TO ASSEMBLE AND PRESENT:
Additional 2 Tablespoons
  unsalted butter
½ cup brandy, warmed

Serves 8
Sixteen to twenty 5″
  cooked dessert crêpes
  (use recipe for "Classic
  Dessert Crêpe Batter")

Into pan over medium heat, put butter, orange juice and lemon juice, Cointreau and Grand Marnier liqueurs. Bring to boil. Remove pan from heat. Add honey or sugar and orange zest. Remember this mixture may be kept in a jar, refrigerated, for a long time.

Into shallow pan or skillet over medium-high heat, place 1-2 teaspoons butter. Fold each crêpe (according to the directions in essay) and lay as many as possible flat in the pan. Spoon sauce over them and heat. When sauce is just bubbly, add brandy and ignite. (Have cover of pan nearby in case flame gets out of control.) Serve hot with more of the warmed sauce spooned over crêpes. Repeat process until all crêpes are used, or until no one wants any more. Unlikely.

Elizabeth's Crêpes Beignets
with Brandy Marmalade

Elizabeth has been my girl Friday for *Denver Delicious.* As chief cook and bottle washer, not to mention research assistant, she personifies the new generation of talented cooks coming along. Nothing is too much trouble for them to prepare in the kitchen when assured (well almost) of spectacular results.

Beignets are deep-fried crêpes, more often seen in restaurants than in private homes. But they taste so fantastic and look so enticing that you had better believe they are well worth adding to your repertoire. Beignets are an ingenious way to use leftover crêpes.

TO MAKE BEIGNETS:
Twelve cooked 5" basic dessert crêpes (use recipe for "Classic Dessert Crêpe Batter")
1½-2 cups safflower or peanut oil
¼ cup powdered sugar, sifted

FOR THE BRANDY MARMALADE:
8 oz. orange marmalade
1 oz. brandy

Serves 8

Pour oil into deep pan and heat over high heat (350°).

Cut crêpes into 1½" strips. When fat is sizzling, fry a handful of crêpe strips at a time, until light brown. Drain on brown paper. Sprinkle with powdered sugar. Serve hot or at room temperature with Brandy Marmalade.

Heat marmalade and brandy in small pan. Pour into small dish. Serve warm as a dip for beignets.

Gâteau of Crêpes

When you have a treasure in your freezer, a stack of well-wrapped crêpes, here is a splashy dessert which can be assembled in jiffy time. In fact, if you wish, you may make it weeks ahead of time, and keep the entire dessert in the freezer for an interminable length of time.

Whether it is a French gâteau or an American "cake", visualize this dessert in its cake-like splendor, and let your imagination rip to decide which ice cream and which trimmings appeal most to you. For instance, use cut up small marshmallows, nuts, hard candies or crushed caramels, etc. All combine well with ice cream.

8 large cooked 7″ dessert crêpes (use recipe for "Classic Dessert Crêpe Batter")
1½ pts.-1 qt. ice cream (your favorite flavor—mine is bitter-sweet chocolate), softened
½-¾ cup chopped nuts
One package small marshmallows, diced

Serves 10-12

Place one crêpe flat on tray. Spread crêpe with just-softened ice cream. It is very important that ice cream not be runny. Ice cream can be mixed with nuts and marshmallows, or whatever is your choice.

Top with another crêpe, and spread again with the ice cream or ice cream mixture. Cover with still another crêpe and ice cream. Continue until all crêpes are used. Cover entire cake with additional ice cream. Place Gâteau of Crêpes in freezer immediately to become firm.

Before serving, let Gâteau soften a bit so that guests will not break their spoons when they dive in. Not to mention their teeth.

Lemon Soufflé Crêpes

If you swoon for both soufflés and crêpes, Lemon Soufflé Crêpes are right up your whisk. The combined texture of the crisp but fragile crêpes with the puffy, soft lemon soufflé is to die for. This has to be the ultimate crêpe recipe. When you perfect it, you will have arrived as a notable cook.

Because of its fragility, this dessert has to be served soonest.

2 Tablespoons unsalted butter
3 Tablespoon unbleached flour
⅓ cup milk, warmed
2 eggs
1 Tablespoon honey, warmed,
 or 2 Tablespoons superfine
 sugar
2 Tablespoons fresh
 lemon juice*
2 teaspoons grated lemon zest
2 teaspoons powdered sugar,
 sifted
20 cooked dessert crêpes
 (see recipe for "Basic
 Dessert Crêpe Batter")
2 teaspoons pure lemon extract
 or additional 2 teaspoons
 fresh lemon juice

One very long shallow pan,
 buttered

FOR THE TOPPING:
Additional 1 Tablespoon
 powdered sugar, sifted

*If lemon is dry, place in a slow oven about ten minutes before juicing. Juice will be more than doubled.

Serves 8

Preheat oven to 425°.

In pan over medium-low heat, melt butter. Whisk in flour. Cook 2 minutes, as you whisk constantly. Remove pan from heat. Continue to whisk as you add warmed milk gradually. Return pan to heat. Cook as you stir constantly, until mixture thickens. Pour into large bowl. Beat in egg yolks, one at a time. Add honey or sugar, lemon juice and zest. Cool.

In a separate bowl, beat egg whites. Gradually add 2 teaspoons powdered sugar and beat until egg whites are stiff and glossy. Fold one-third beaten egg whites into lemon mixture. Gently fold in remaining egg whites.

Lay one cooked crêpe flat on working surface. The browner side of the crêpe should be on the bottom, so this better side is exposed to view when rolled up. Spoon about 1 Tablespoon lemon soufflé mixture into center of crêpe. Carefully roll up prepared crêpe. Repeat with remaining crêpes. Arrange crêpes in baking pan. Lightly brush tops with 2 teaspoons lemon extract or lemon juice. Place pan in oven 8 to 10 minutes. Crêpes should be warm and soufflé puffy, rather than runny.

Just before serving, lightly sprinkle additional powdered sugar over tops of crêpes.

Pear and Ginger Crêpes Flambées

Pear and ginger make an irresistible duet. Combined with dessert crêpes, and all flamed with brandy, they become an exciting dessert. If you have heeded my advice and have a pile of crêpes made and stashed away in your freezer, the making of the filling, and the assembling and reheating the crêpes is a breeze. Your guests will be overcome with awe.

6 medium-size pears
Juice of half lemon
½ cup honey
¾ cup crystallized ginger, slivered
1½ Tablespoons brandy

Serves 8
Two filled dessert crêpes for each serving.

Core, peel and halve pears. As you prepare each pear, drop it quickly into a bowl of cold water with lemon juice added to preserve color.

Place honey in pan over medium heat to warm, not boil. Remove pears from water and pat dry with paper towels. Slice pears. Add to honey. Add ginger and pour in brandy. Reduce heat to simmer. Cook, uncovered, for about 30 minutes until gooey and slightly thick.

Preheat broiler to medium.

Take one crêpe and lay better side down flat on working surface. Spoon about 1½ Tablespoons pear-ginger mixture into center of crêpe and roll up. Repeat to fill all crêpes. As each crêpe is filled, place in pan.

Place pan under medium broiler about 6 minutes until crêpes are heated and bubbly.

Place crêpes in a dish or bowl that has some depth. Pour warmed brandy over crêpes and ignite. Bring flaming dish to table.

TO ASSEMBLE:
16 cooked dessert crêpes
(can have brandy in batter)
at room temperature

One rectangular pan,
preferably oven-to-table,
lightly oiled

TO PRESENT:

Mile-High Soufflés

Chapter VI

Tricks Make the Difference

Many cooks share an inferiority complex about creating a hot soufflé. Needless to fret when you learn these tricks. The soufflé is the irresistible prima donna of the culinary world. Nothing will please your guests more than to wait for their—and your, by the way,—soufflé to rise!

Since soufflés spring from the French cuisine, the word itself is derived from the French verb "souffler", meaning to breathe or to inflate. As an accomplished cook, your goal is to serve a soufflé boasting a high rise. Because soufflés are evanescent, a soufflé must be served the moment it is removed from the oven. The old saw is that guests wait for the soufflé—the soufflé never waits for the guests. If you heed a few directions, you, too, will be able to make the perfect soufflé every time.

Remember there are two kinds of soufflés: savory and dessert. Savory soufflés are ones with cheese, vegetables, and infinite combinations of meat, poultry or fish, with or without vegetables. They may be served as a main course for a luncheon or supper, sometimes for a fancy brunch. As a first course, they are hard to beat and they set the stage for a marvelous dinner to follow. Serving soufflés first generates a certain electricity and the action starts. Also, serving a savory soufflé as a first course is less worrisome to the host's/hostess's time table, since the guests can be called to table just a few minutes before the soufflé leaves the oven.

Dessert soufflés, when perfectly executed, like the popular Grand Marnier one, chocolate, orange or an infinite number of flavors, remain the star in a cook's firmament. Nothing can touch a high-rise soufflé.

But don't feel guilty if you don't want the strain of producing a hot soufflé at an exact moment, because cold soufflés, which can be made ahead, are also a sensual delight. It is comforting to the cook to know that an exquisite cold soufflé is happily ensconced in the refrigerator waiting to be served whenever. No matter which type of soufflé you plan to serve and at what temperature, there are universal tricks which once you grasp them, should not only jet propel you to try making soufflés, but to serve them often for awed compliments from your guests. Once you learn these ground rules, you'll understand the principles and be able to concoct a soufflé quickly and easily; believe it or not.

Choosing the Proper Soufflé Dish

One of the reasons so many cooks attract disaster from their soufflés is that too large a dish is chosen, with too large a surface. The smaller your dish, the better your chances of success for a soufflé with a high rise.

For a small dessert soufflé serving 4, using 3 eggs and an extra egg white, use a 4-or-5-cup dish. For a larger soufflé using 6 eggs and two additional egg whites, use a 6-cup (1½-qt.) dish. Don't test your luck by using a 3-qt. dish. Rather, if you have 8 guests, make two soufflés. Another point to remember when choosing a soufflé dish, always use a straight sided, rather than curvaceous, dish. (I learned this the hard way.)

Both glass and ceramic soufflé dishes in varied sizes are for sale everywhere. Also, do not overlook charlotte molds which can easily double for soufflé dishes. Charlotte molds have a sneaky advantage as they do not need collaring. But I still prefer a glass soufflé dish which allows you to see a soufflé's breathtaking evolution.

Preparing the Soufflé Dish

Once you have settled on which soufflé dish(es) you are using and once you have washed it to make sure it is spotlessly clean, prepare the dish for baking. (It is unnecessary to butter and coat the dish for a cold soufflé.) To prepare the dish for a dessert soufflé, first melt about 1 to 2 Tablespoons unsalted butter in a glass measuring cup. Place cup in microwave about 20-30 seconds at full power. Remember, butter will continue to melt even after it is removed from microwave. If you don't have a microwave oven, place cup in small pan of boiling water on stove and watch until butter melts. Melting time will depend on the amount of butter, the temperature of the water and the heat of the burner. Then, with a clean pastry brush, cover every inch of the dish with melted butter. When this is completed, drizzle about ½ cup sugar onto dish to coat thoroughly bottom and sides of dish. After sugar has coated the butter, take the dish in your hands and rotate it until lightly and evenly coated. If you see any unbuttered and uncoated spots, repair them quickly as soufflé will adhere to them. This prevents your ideal high rise.

To prepare dish for a chocolate soufflé, coat dish with cocoa instead of sugar for better color.

To prepare dish for a savory soufflé, use plain butter and flour to coat the dish, but copy the same method. Coating the dish with the same kind of cheese you are using in the soufflé is a splendid touch.

No matter if your coating is sugar, cocoa, flour or cheese, shake out all the excess coating in dish by turning it upside down and giving it a whack on the bottom. Otherwise, you'll have lumps inside the dish, which will hinder the soufflé's rising to its maximum.

Refrigerate the prepared soufflé dish, as a very cold dish helps the soufflé to rise straight.

Collaring the Soufflé Dish

After the soufflé dish is buttered and coated, decide whether or not it will need a collar as reinforcement. If you are at present a novice at making soufflés, a collar is a wise precaution. Of course, a collar holds the risen part of the soufflé and should be removed just before serving. Collars are usually for dishes containing cold soufflés and also are used for all sizes of soufflé dishes, except for individual soufflé dishes where collars are normally unnecessary.

This is how you construct a collar using either wax paper or aluminum foil: measure the circumference of the dish and add three to four inches. Tear or cut waxed paper or foil to that length. Fold the width in half. Butter and coat the inside half slightly. Place the collar-to-be with prepared side facing inward around outside of the top of the dish. It should extend about 2½ inches above the rim. Secure collar with a length of string tied taut around collar to hold it in place.

Eggs at Room Temperature

Be sure always to use extra-large eggs. In order to achieve the most volume from beaten egg whites, they should always be at room temperature before beating them. So try to remember to remove eggs from your refrigerator at least 2 hours before starting a soufflé.

What happens when you come home from work late, or you just feel in the mood to make a soufflé at the last minute? Simply place refrigerated eggs in a bowl of warm water to warm gently. Don't go overboard by having the water too hot, or leaving the eggs too long, as they will begin to cook. That is a no-no. So feel the eggs from time to time and remove them from the warm water as soon as they reach room temperature.

Making the Basic Soufflé Mixture
(Panade or Pastry Cream)

Usually a panade is the basic mixture for a savory soufflé, while pastry cream is the basic mixture for a dessert soufflé. Although a panade and pastry cream are similar, the method of making them differs.

For aid to less experienced cooks, and for less frustration for all levels of cooks, opt for making the panade in the top of a double boiler. First, melt the butter. When butter is hot and foamy, whisk in flour. Cook two to three minutes to eradicate once and for all the unpleasant taste of raw flour. Add the liquid (milk, cream, or stock) gradually and slowly as you whisk away.

Remove top of double boiler from heat and whisk in egg yolks, one at a time. Add main flavoring ingredient. Experienced cooks will recognize this panade as a thick Béchamel sauce. Return top of double boiler to heat and whisk mixture three to four minutes. The panade should be smooth and the texture thick like mayonnaise.

The technique of making the pastry cream—the first step in creating a dessert soufflé—is to first bring milk to a boil. Whisk together sugar with egg yolks in a separate bowl. Whisk in flour until blended. When milk boils, pour it slowly over egg yolk mixture as you continue to whisk until well mixed. Pour entire mixture into top of double boiler over high heat, and continue to whisk vigorously. Pastry cream will thicken. Continue to stir a minute or two. Add flavoring and mix. Pastry cream should be free from lumps and resemble thick mayonnaise.

Both a panade and a pastry cream can be made in advance. Cover top of mixture with a round of waxed paper to prevent a skin from forming. Refrigerate.

Also, be sure to remember that either a panade or pastry cream needs to be warm, not hot nor cool, before beaten egg whites are added. So if you have refrigerated the panade or pastry cream or allowed either to cool, heat either slightly. Then it will be ready to accept the stiffly beaten egg whites, rather than offering them a cold shoulder.

Preheating Oven

Plopping a carefully prepared soufflé in its dish into a cold oven is courting trouble. Rather, turn oven on to desired temperature to preheat just as you start beating the egg whites. My relatively new oven takes 10 minutes to preheat, but your oven make take a shorter or longer period, so check yours. In any event, it is essential to preheat your oven for optimum soufflé making.

Of course, should you be baking your soufflé in a show-off convection oven where everyone can see the soufflé rise because of the oven's glass doors and top, there is no need to preheat. Saves energy, too.

Beating Egg Whites

Well-beaten egg whites at room temperature are the main secret of producing a spectacular soufflé. Another checkpoint is making certain the bowl and whisk you intend to use are spotlessly clean, free from grease.

Separating cold eggs is far easier than separating warm eggs; so if this worries you, separate eggs when they are cold, but don't put egg whites into a metal or copper bowl until you are ready to beat them. Unbeaten egg whites must not have one fleck of egg yolk or shell, so pluck any out (with half egg shell, spoon or finger) if you have even a speck.

Each cook has his favorite way of beating egg whites. The copper bowl and balloon whisk increase the volume of beaten egg whites the most, but if your arm is not up to that strenuous beating, an electric mixer (use only with minimum of 3 egg whites), or electric hand beater is a fine substitute. Adding ¼ teaspoon cream of tartar for every 4 egg whites accomplishes a similar chemical reaction to the one produced by copper with egg whites. Sometimes a pinch of salt is added in place of the cream of tartar.

Another way to stabilize beaten egg whites is to add about 2 Table-spoons superfine sugar, reserved from amount of sugar listed under ingredients. Add sugar gradually when egg whites are just peaking.

The best beaten egg whites for a soufflé should be glossy and moist. The acid test to ascertain whether or not they have been beaten long enough is to turn the bowl holding the egg whites upside down. If the egg whites remain stationary, they have passed the test with flying colors, and are ready to incorporate into the basic soufflé mixture.

One small caution: avoid doing what comes naturally to many a cook: never hit egg beaters covered with beaten egg whites against the side of bowl holding newly beaten egg whites as the customary terrific whack destroys some of your desired volume, just achieved.

Folding in Beaten Egg Whites

It is of the utmost importance to fold beaten egg whites properly into the warm panade or warm pastry cream. With a rubber spatula, take one-fourth to one-third of stiffly beaten egg whites and blend gently and swiftly into basic soufflé mixture to lighten it. Fold in beaten egg whites by moving spatula downward gently through the center of the soufflé mixture. Come forward with spatula to circle the edges of the bowl, as you rotate it, a quarter turn at a time. Repeat this procedure rapidly a few times until mixture is fairly well blended. Spread remaining egg whites on top of soufflé mixture. Repeat identical movements with spatula until soufflé mixture is incorporated into egg whites. Streaks of white should be visible.

Pouring Soufflé into Dish and Crowning Soufflé

If making a cold soufflé with a collared dish, pour soufflé mixture just to the top of the dish itself and refrigerate until barely firm. (Simultaneously, refrigerate leftover soufflé mixture in bowl.) When chilled soufflé in dish is firm, layer remaining reserved soufflé, contained by the collar, on top of chilled soufflé.

When a hot or cold soufflé is poured into a collarless dish, level it off at once by scraping across the top with a knife and dumping the excess. Pity, unless the cook wants a taste.

No doubt in restaurants you have admired extravagantly a soufflé with a hat or a crown. This is easily achieved by running your knife around the middle of the soufflé in the dish before placing it in oven. Make a circle halfway between the center and the outside edge, and touching the bottom of the dish with your knife, cut through the soufflé all the way around.

As a precaution against soufflés sticking to the dish anywhere I, also before baking, run my knife around the entire outer edge of the inside of the dish, again from the bottom through the whole soufflé mixture to the very top.

Flexibility of Soufflés

Much to many cooks' amazement, soufflés are not completely fragile and are a bit more flexible than once advised. As previously said, the basic mixture for a hot soufflé can be made ahead and warmed just before incorporating beaten egg whites.

Or, if you wish to prepare the whole soufflé and pour it into its dish, you can safely refrigerate it three to four hours. In that case, put it directly into the preheated oven, rather than letting it return to room temperature first. Add a short additional baking time, depending on how cold the soufflé is.

Courageous cooks even leave a completely baked soufflé in the oven up to 10 minutes before serving it. Turn oven off, but leave oven door tightly shut. Let it rest in peace.

Creating cold soufflés is a cinch, requiring no magic whatsoever. Happily, they can be made ahead and refrigerated several hours before serving.

Baking a Soufflé

Place soufflé in dish on middle rack of preheated oven and follow exact directions for time of baking specified in individual recipes. Don't dare peek nor walk too heavily right in front of oven door, as soufflés don't care to be jiggled.

As a dessert soufflé is snatched from the oven and when you are not napping it with a sauce, you may wish to sift some powdered sugar over the top. An ingenious way to do this is to use a paper doily, the same size as the top of the soufflé dish, and hold it over the soufflé. As you sift the powdered sugar through the doily, an enchanting lacey design is produced.

Some diners, however, will invariably prefer a crustier and more well-done soufflé. Each to his taste. Test to see if soufflé is done with an inserted skewer or long toothpick (you can open oven door by now!), and if necessary, return soufflé to oven, usually with a lowered temperature. A soufflé cooked longer is less apt to collapse.

Carving a Soufflé Adroitly

All systems are GO. The soufflé has to be served immediately after removal from oven. You have a breathing time of only four minutes. Remove collar quickly if there is one.

Carving a soufflé correctly preserves your work of art and makes you an instant admired chef; but no need to make a production of it, it's easy to do. Take two implements such as a large spoon and fork or, as I prefer, a cake cutter and spoon. Hold them back to back. Plunge them into your soufflé and cut like a pie, but lift up. (Should you make the error of using a downward stroke, the soufflé will deflate even more.)

Dole out to each eager guest his fair share of the soufflé, expertly and rapidly. After all, a soufflé is hot air and, like a balloon, it will always burst quickly.

Beet Soufflé

So often when cooks and/or diners dream about a soufflé, it is a golden soufflé, be it cheese or Grand Marnier. Vegetable soufflés are nothing to be sneezed at. High on my list of favorites is Beet Soufflé, combining an incredible shade of carmine with a feathery texture and sublime flavor.

Beet Soufflé is simple to make, once you know how, even though your guests will think you contrived it with hocus-pocus.

2-2½ bunches fresh beets (quantity depends on size of beets), cooked (reserve cooking water), peeled
2 Tablespoons chives, minced
3 Tablespoons fresh dill leaves, minced or
1 Tablespoon dried dill leaves
Salt and pepper, freshly ground, to taste
¾ cup plain yogurt
¾ cup sour cream
5 eggs, separated

One 8-cup (2 qt.) soufflé dish, unbuttered

Serves 8

Preheat oven to 325°.

In food processor bowl fitted with steel blade, place cut up beets around blades. Process to purée. Scrape down bowl two separate times with plastic scraper and add a small amount of water beets were cooked in (1 Tablespoon will suffice) to purée. Add herbs and seasonings. Process briefly to blend.

Remove puréed beets to another bowl. With rubber spatula, quickly and carefully fold in yogurt and sour cream.

Beat egg yolks until thick and lemon colored. Gradually add them to beet mixture as you stir to combine.

Beat egg whites until stiff and glossy. With rubber spatula, fold one-third of beaten egg whites into beet mixture. Gently and quickly fold in remaining beaten egg whites. Pour into soufflé dish. Bake 35 minutes. Serve hot immediately.

116

Fish Soufflé

One of the unheralded joys of a savory soufflé's versatility is to incorporate and thus recycle your leftovers. Who wants to eat cold fish the next day? But leftover fish, disguised in a soufflé, becomes part of a memorable creation.

You may use fresh, frozen or canned fish, even if it is not a leftover. But when using frozen or canned fish, be sure it is thoroughly drained, as excess liquid can play havoc with your soufflé.

Of course, should you wish to substitute leftover meat or poultry in place of the fish as an ingredient, there is no problem. Just change the name of the soufflé, and everything else fits.

6 oz. fish
2 Tablespoons butter
2 Tablespoons unbleached flour
1 cup less 2 Tablespoons
  milk
Salt and white pepper
  to taste
⅛ teaspoon cayenne
2 oz. sharp Cheddar cheese,
  grated
4 eggs

One 4 cup (1-qt.) soufflé dish,
  buttered and coated with
  cheese (or flour)

Serves 6-8

Preheat oven to 375°.

Over low heat, melt butter. Whisk in flour to make roux. Cook 3 to 4 minutes. Gradually add milk, as you stir continuously, until sauce thickens and comes to a boil. Season with salt and white pepper. Add cayenne. Stir in cheese. Remove pan from heat and let sauce cool at least 5 minutes.

Separate eggs. Add egg yolks, one at a time, to cheese mixture as you stir after each addition. Flake the fish finely with fork and blend it into sauce. Correct seasoning, if necessary.

Beat egg whites until stiff, not dry. With rubber spatula, fold one-third of beaten egg whites into fish mixture and then swiftly fold in remaining beaten egg whites. Pour mixture into prepared soufflé dish. Bake on middle rack about 35 minutes until soufflé has risen and has a crusty golden brown top. Test to see if top is springy. Serve hot at once.

Make-Ahead Cheese Soufflé

An astonishing soufflé because of its flexibility. Take your choice: make it and bake at once, or refrigerate it up to 18 hours, or freeze it up to 7 days. Of course, baking time will be increased when soufflé is refrigerated or frozen; additional time depends on how cold soufflé is. Place it into oven immediately; no need to return it to room temperature first.

Even more astonishing, no matter which way you choose to execute Make-Ahead Cheese Soufflé, the soufflé will emerge with a pleasant rise and crusty top over a supremely textured cheese soufflé. Certainly, your guests will avow you did it all at the last minute, and who's to know?

12 oz. sharp cheddar cheese (about 3¼ cups shredded) cut up
6 Tablespoons butter
6 Tablespoons flour
1½ cups milk
1 teaspoon salt
½ teaspoon paprika
¼ teaspoon cayenne
¼ teaspoon dry mustard
1 teaspoon Worcestershire sauce
6 eggs, separated

One 8-cup (2-qt.) soufflé dish, oiled and floured, then refrigerated

Serves 8

Preheat oven to 325°.

With food processor bowl fitted with shredder, add cheese through feed tube. With medium pressure, process briefly to shred cheese.

In a double boiler, melt butter and whisk in flour to make roux. Add milk gradually. Add salt, paprika, cayenne, dry mustard and Worcestershire sauce. Taste mixture and adjust seasonings. Add cheese and stir until mixture is smooth and thickened.

Beat egg yolks until thick and lemon colored. Gradually stir egg yolks into cheese mixture. Beat egg whites until stiff, not dry. With a rubber spatula, fold one-third of beaten egg whites into cheese mixture, and then, gently fold in remaining egg whites. Do not overbeat.

Pour into prepared soufflé dish. Bake 35 to 45 minutes or until puffed and golden. Remember, baking time is increased if soufflé has just been removed from refrigerator or freezer.

Miner's Souffléed Omelet

No one knows for sure whether a Colorado miner took greater pleasure from contemplating a gold strike or consuming this light golden souffléed omelet, sprinkled with diced ham. Let's call it a tie.

4 oz. ham
2 Tablespoons butter
4 bread slices
Salt and pepper, freshly ground, to taste
5 eggs at room temperature
2 parsley sprigs, stemmed, minced

One 3½" deep ovenproof dish, at least 8" × 8", oiled

Serves 4

Preheat oven to 400°.

Dice ham. In skillet, sauté ham in 1 Tablespoon sizzling butter until ham is crisp. Remove ham but keep warm. Reserve skillet.

Butter bread slices on both sides with remaining 1 Tablespoon butter. Sauté in same skillet. Turn over each bread slice to sauté on both sides. Salt and pepper.

Separate eggs. Beat yolks with fork. Beat egg whites until firm, not dry, and glossy. Fold yolks carefully and rapidly into beaten egg whites.

In prepared ovenproof dish, place bread slices side-by-side. Pour egg mixture over bread. Scatter diced ham on top. Bake 10 minutes. Sprinkle minced parsley around ham. Serve Miner's Souffléed Omelet hot, immediately.

Never-Fail Cheese Soufflé

When any novice cook asks me for an easy recipe for a soufflé that never misses, Never-Fail Cheese Soufflé is invariably my choice. Unbelievably, it can wait in the oven an additional hour when you opt for the 2 hour baking time.

This Never-Fail Cheese Soufflé can be served as a tantalizing first course for a party dinner, a main dish for a luncheon, or a spiffy accompaniment to meat, poultry, or fish. No matter how you choose to serve it, your cooking reputation will soar.

If there is any left over, refrigerate it. Amazingly, it is still good heated the next day—especially as an underpinning for any creamed dish, made with, for instance, leftover turkey or ham.

2 oz. Swiss cheese
  (about ½ cup grated)
2 oz. Parmesan cheese
  (about ½ cup grated)
3 Tablespoons butter
3 Tablespoons flour
1⅞ cups milk
1 teaspoon salt (optional)
⅛ teaspoon cayenne
1 teaspoon dry mustard
3-4 drops Worcestershire
  sauce
6 eggs, separated

One 8-cup (2-qt.) soufflé
  dish, oiled, coated
  with cheese

Serves 6 as first course
Serves 4 as main course

Preheat oven to 350°.

With food processor bowl fitted with shredder, add cut up cheeses through feed tube. With medium pressure, process to grate. Reserve.

In double boiler over high heat, melt butter and whisk in flour gradually until slightly thickened to make roux. Add milk, salt, cayenne, dry mustard and Worcestershire sauce. Blend and cook mixture over high heat, as you stir continuously. Add grated cheese and cook until absorbed. Remove pan from heat and cool slightly to warm.

Beat egg yolks until thick and add cheese mixture, as you stir constantly. In another bowl, beat egg whites until stiff and glossy. Fold into cheese mixture. Pour into prepared soufflé dish. Bake one hour in preheated 350° oven, or you may bake this Never-Fail Cheese Soufflé in a preheated 300° oven 2 hours.

Zucchini Pudding Soufflé
with Tomato Sauce

Like so many recipes Denverites use, this prize was brought to Denver by a student cook of a master French chef. It embodies two separate cooking processes: first, it is cooked in a bain-marie (hot water bath) for its first puff; after it is inverted on a heated platter, the soufflé is masked with Tomato Sauce and cheese, and gratinéed in hot oven to again inflate. This soufflé is the epitome of all vegetable soufflés.

1 lb. small, firm zucchini
Salt to extract
  moisture from zucchini
3 Tablespoons butter
3 Tablespoons flour
¾ cup milk
3 eggs, separated
Salt and pepper, freshly
  ground, to taste

One 6-cup (1½-qt.) ring mold,
  heavily oiled

FOR THE TOMATO SAUCE:
⅔ cup tomato purée
  (preferably homemade)
1 cup heavy cream

FOR THE TOPPING:
½ cup Parmesan cheese,
  freshly grated

Serves 4
(For 8, make twice)

Preheat oven to 350°.

With food processor bowl fitted with shredder, use light pressure on pusher to coarsely shred the zucchini. Layer zucchini in a large mixing bowl; sprinkle each layer with salt. Leave for ½ hour, then squeeze with your hands to press out moisture. Squeeze tightly and repeatedly between both hands until you can no longer wring out any more liquid. Dump excess liquid in sink or save for your stock pot.

Melt 1 Tablespoon butter in heavy skillet over medium heat. Sauté zucchini 7 to 8 minutes, until well dried and lightly colored.

Melt remaining 2 Tablespoons butter in a pan. Whisk in flour and cook as you stir until frothy and bubbling. Add milk gradually. Whisk until sauce boils and thickens. Remove from heat. Cool a few minutes and then add egg yolks, one at a time. Stir well after each addition. Season to taste with salt and pepper. Stir in zucchini. Beat egg whites until soft peaks form. Fold one-third of egg whites into the zucchini mixture, then fold in remaining egg whites.

Pour soufflé mixture into prepared ring mold. Smooth surface with rubber spatula. Tap mold slightly to settle contents. Put mold into a larger pan holding hot water, so water comes two-thirds up the mold's outside (bain-marie). Bake about 30 minutes until top feels firm and springy. Remove mold from oven

(continued on next page)

and cool for 10 minutes. Run thin knife around edges of mold to loosen soufflé. Put large ovenproof plate or platter on top of mold and invert. Give it a whack so soufflé unmolds onto dish perfectly.

Raise oven temperature to 450°.

Whisk together tomato purée and cream. Season to taste. Pour tomato sauce over soufflé, masking it entirely. Sprinkle with Parmesan cheese and bake in oven additional 20 minutes. Serve soufflé on heated individual plates with the sauce spooned over sides.

Chocolate Magical Puff Soufflé

An oft-forgotten technique for making fail-safe soufflés is to use the trusty double boiler instead of the oven. Begin the cooking period for this recipe as you commence serving your main course and your timing will be faultless. This recipe is easy and Chocolate Magical Puff Soufflé remains exceptionally delicious year in, year out. The texture is truly magical. Guests sigh.

7 oz. semi-sweet chocolate
  morsels
1⅓ cups milk
2 Tablespoons honey, warmed,
  or 3 Tablespoons sugar
1 teaspoon vanilla
3 eggs

GARNISH: (optional)
1 cup whipped cream

Serves 8

Place chocolate morsels and milk in top of double boiler over high heat. Stir as chocolate melts. Add honey or sugar, vanilla and eggs. Beat together briefly (2-3 minutes). Cover top of double boiler and cook over boiling water about 25 minutes without peeking.

Remove double boiler from heat and serve at once. Crown with whipped cream, if you must.

Chocolate Soufflé à la Blanding

Sarah Blanding officiated as the first lady president of my alma mater, Vassar College. Distinguished as an administrator, she was also adept at hostessing. In her well-chosen words: *"My recipe for Chocolate Soufflé is easy to make, mouth melting and guests will always lap it up."*

Besides underscoring her words, I can testify that this recipe has been a mainstay at our house for 25 years.

1 cup milk
2 Tablespoons unsalted butter
2 Tablespoons flour
⅜ cup honey, warmed,
  or ¾ cup superfine sugar
⅛ teaspoon salt
1½ oz. (1½ squares)
  unsweetened chocolate
1 teaspoon vanilla
4 eggs, separated

One 6-cup (1½-qt.) soufflé dish,
  buttered, coated with cocoa

Serves 8

Preheat oven to 350°.

In double boiler over high heat, heat milk. In another pan, over low heat, combine melted butter with flour. Pour a little warm milk over butter-flour mixture and stir. Add remaining milk and when mixed, return milk mixture to double boiler. Add warmed honey or sugar, salt and chocolate. (No need to grate the chocolate, just stir like fury until chocolate melts.) Remove pan from stove and cool mixture to lukewarm. Add vanilla.

Beat egg yolks until thickened and lemony. Add them to cooled chocolate mixture and combine. Beat egg whites until stiff and glossy. With rubber spatula, fold in one-third beaten egg whites. Add remaining beaten egg whites. Pour into prepared soufflé dish. Bake about 30 minutes, but check after 20 minutes.

Rick's Grand Marnier Chocolate Soufflé

Credit Rick Grausman from the Cordon Bleu of Paris, for bringing innumerable superb dishes to Denver. High among these is this versatile double whammy Grand Marnier and chocolate soufflé—which can be baked at once or refrigerated or frozen and then baked. Take your choice but always increase baking time when either refrigerated or frozen beforehand. Rick advises making this soufflé without flour, as chocolate is the thickening agent.

To explore further the versatility of this soufflé: you can serve it uncooked as a chocolate mousse. For an occasional live-it-up dessert, line a buttered soufflé dish with lady fingers around the sides and then pour in the uncooked mixture and refrigerate or deep freeze until the boss comes unexpectedly to dinner. You'll assuredly receive a raise.

6 oz. semi-sweet chocolate
6 Tablespoons unsalted butter
6 eggs, separated
Grated zest of one orange
3 Tablespoons Grand Marnier
  liqueur

One 6-cup (1½-qt.) soufflé dish,
  buttered and coated with
  sugar

Serves 6-8

Preheat oven to 475°.

In double boiler over medium heat, place chocolate and butter. When mixture is melted, remove pan from heat. Stir in beaten egg yolks. Pour into large mixing bowl. Flavor with grated orange zest and Grand Marnier.

Beat egg whites until stiff and glossy. With rubber spatula, fold one-third beaten egg whites into chocolate mixture. Fold in remaining egg whites. Pour into prepared soufflé dish. Bake 5 minutes. Turn oven temperature down to 425°. Bake an additional 5 to 7 minutes. If serving immediately, dust with powdered sugar.

Snowy Cream Cheese Soufflé with Brandied Black Cherry Sauce

A novel, but comparatively easy soufflé that is a show-off because of the snowy white color of the soufflé accentuated by the dark cherry sauce. The texture is midway between that of a soufflé and a cheese cake, and the soufflé boasts an admirable rise. What's more: the prepared soufflé can survive up to four hours in the refrigerator before baking, but increase baking time an additional 5 to 10 minutes.

10½ oz. cream cheese, softened
1⅓ cups sour cream*
1½ Tablespoons honey,
  warmed
¼ teaspoon salt (optional)
5 eggs, separated
2-3 Tablespoons superfine
  sugar

One 6-cup (1½-qt.) soufflé dish,
  buttered and coated with
  sugar

*⅔ cup yogurt may be substituted for 1⅓ cups sour cream to reduce calories, but texture will not be as great nor will the original snowy color be preserved. Also, do not process yogurt with food processor. Rather, reserve yogurt and add gently to egg yolk mixture with rubber spatula.

**FOR THE BRANDIED
  BLACK CHERRY SAUCE:**
1 cup orange juice
3 Tablespoons arrowroot
⅓ cup water
One 16 ½-oz. can black
  cherries with syrup
4 Tablespoons brandy

Serves 8
Preheat oven to 375°.

Into food processor bowl fitted with metal blade, place cut up cheese around blades. Process briefly. Add sour cream, just-warmed honey, salt (optional) and process until barely mixed. With motor running, add egg yolks, one at a time, through feed tube. Process. Remove to separate bowl.

Beat egg whites until peaked. Incorporate sugar gradually. With rubber spatula, take one-third of beaten egg whites and quickly blend into cheese mixture. Fold in remaining egg whites. Pour into prepared soufflé dish. Bake about 30 minutes, but check after 25 minutes.

Yield: 3½ cups
In top of double boiler, heat orange juice. Dissolve arrowroot in measuring cup with water to cover. Add to orange juice. Cook mixture until thick. Add cherries with syrup. Continue cooking until mixture is thoroughly heated. Remove double boiler from heat. (Sauce may be refrigerated at this point.)

Add brandy. Serve sauce hot (you may need to reheat) or cold over Snowy Cream Cheese Soufflé.

Soufflé Grand Marnier

This tasteful creamy Grand Marnier Soufflé—which soufflés unusually high—makes an enchanting summer dessert! Actually not too bad all year around.

1-2 Tablespoons butter, melted* and sugar to coat soufflé dish
4-5 egg yolks
⅓ cup sugar
¼ cup Grand Marnier liqueur
5 egg whites
¼ teaspoon cream of tartar**

One 6-cup (1½-qt.) soufflé dish, buttered, coated with sugar

*In microwave, 1-2 Tablespoons butter can be quickly melted in glass measuring cup, 15-20 seconds at full strength (100% power).

**Omit cream of tartar when beating eggs in a copper bowl.

Serves 4-6

Preheat oven to 450°.

Coat soufflé dish with melted butter (use pastry brush) and sugar. If you miss a spot, the soufflé will stick.

With an electric hand mixer, beat egg yolks with sugar in top of a double boiler over medium heat until the mixture, dropped from a spoon, forms a ribbon. Stir in Grand Marnier. Remove double boiler from stove and place it over a bowl of cracked ice to cool contents.

Beat egg whites with cream of tartar until firm not dry. With rubber spatula, fold whites, one-third at a time, quickly and gently into Grand Marnier mixture. Pour into prepared soufflé dish and bake 12 to 15 minutes, until soufflé rises and is delicately browned. Serve hot immediately.

To make this Soufflé Grand Marnier at higher altitudes such as Vail's, use only 4 Tablespoons sugar instead of ⅓ cup. (Reserve 1 Tablespoon). Use ⅓ cup Grand Marnier, instead of ¼ cup. When beaten egg white peak, add the reserved Tablespoon sugar to stabilize them. Continue beating until they hold their shape.

Speedy Lemon Soufflé

Have you ever needed a soufflé recipe that was quick and effortless? This recipe wins my vote for the best soufflé recipe to take on a trip when visiting family or friends and you are responsible at the last minute for whipping up the dessert. Actually, it's not too shabby a dessert to serve at home.

Its flavor—beyond belief—leaves the impression with each fortunate guest that you slaved all day over a hot stove to produce such a masterpiece when, actually, you can make and bake the entire soufflé in 15 to 20 minutes. Who could ask for more?

4 extra large eggs
6 Tablespoons superfine sugar
  (reserve 2 Tablespoons)
Grated zest of one lemon
½ teaspoon pure lemon extract
1 teaspoon Galliano liqueur

One round glass ovenproof
  dish or platter (not to
  exceed 9½″ diameter)

Serves 6

Preheat oven to 475°.

Separate eggs. Beat egg yolks until thick and lemon colored. Add 4 Tablespoons sugar gradually. Beat until well mixed. Add lemon zest and lemon extract. Mix in Galliano.

In another bowl, beat egg whites until peaked. Add reserved 2 Tablespoons sugar gradually. Continue to beat until meringue is stiff. Fold one-third of meringue into lemon mixture gently with rubber spatula. Swiftly and carefully, fold in the remaining meringue.

Mound soufflé mixture on dish or platter (not buttered) with a metal spatula until mixture resembles a small roundish mountain. Place in oven immediately and watch carefully, as it bakes in 4 minutes. Speedy Lemon Soufflé will be a golden hue, but will not rise. Serve at once, and cut judiciously to serve.

Winnie the Pooh's Honey Soufflé in Grapefruit Shells

This is the last word in desserts to serve for a ladies' small committee luncheon. Even though you've researched luncheon dessert recipes for your whole life, you could never top this.

What an ingenious presentation to serve Winnie the Pooh's Honey Soufflé in grapefruit shells, which are usually just tossed into the garbage or left for the compost pile.

Such a celestial souffléed dessert deserves to be served at once, since its height in the shell is terrestial—three whole minutes to be exact. Count them. Pooh Bear would have been in seventh heaven. Maybe even first.

4 egg yolks
⅔ cup honey, warmed
1 teaspoon lemon zest,
  grated
2 Tablespoons flour
2 Tablespoons butter, softened
6 egg whites
2 Tablespoons superfine sugar
8 grapefruit shells from
  4 grapefruit, halved, pulp
  removed (save for breakfast)

One broiler pan

Serves 8

Preheat oven to 375°.

Beat egg yolks until thick and lemon colored. Add barely warmed honey, lemon zest, flour and butter.

Beat egg whites until stiff and glossy. Add sugar gradually and incorporate. Spoon soufflé into each grapefruit shell and mound soufflé on each shell with the back of a tablespoon. (If there is any remaining soufflé, pour it into a separate small prepared soufflé dish, and pop into refrigerator to bake later.) Place mounded grapefruit shells in broiler pan or other large flat pan. Bake 20 minutes or until soufflé turns golden brown and an inserted long toothpick in the center of shell comes out clean. If soufflés are browning too fast, turn oven down to 350°. Serve hot immediately.

Cold Chocolate Brandied Soufflé

A flawless chocolate pudding, but with brandy. As a simple, easy and do-ahead dessert, it is infallible. Served in your prettiest bowl—be it a modern white ceramic or Aunt Minnie's silver or cut-crystal, bring the dish to the table and present it to your salivating guests. Or spoon it into small individual bowls.

Though voluptuous whipped real cream topped with chocolate shavings is a fitting cap for this cold soufflé, Cold Chocolate Brandied Soufflé is a terrific treat alone.

½ cup honey, warmed, or
  ¾ cup superfine sugar
6 eggs, separated
3 oz. semi-sweet chocolate
1 package (1 Tablespoon)
  unflavored gelatin
3 Tablespoons cold water
4 Tablespoons hot water
2 oz. brandy
⅛ teaspoon salt

GARNISH: (optional)
1 cup whipped cream
Additional ½ oz. semi-sweet
  chocolate, grated

Serves 6-8

Beat honey or sugar with egg yolks until thickened and lemon colored. Melt chocolate* and stir into egg yolk mixture. Put gelatin in measuring cup and cover with cold water to dissolve. Add hot water to melt. Add melted gelatin to chocolate mixture.

Beat egg whites until glossy and stiff, not dry. Fold one-third into chocolate mixture. When incorporated, fold in remaining egg whites. Stir in brandy. Add salt. Pour into your prettiest bowl or small individual bowls. Refrigerate at least 2 hours.

If you wish, serve Cold Chocolate Brandied Soufflé with whipped cream amid chocolate shavings.

*Microwave chocolate squares in glass measuring cup 30-40 seconds at simmer (50%).

Iced Raspberry Soufflé

Here is an appealing soufflé to keep in the freezer to serve to unexpected summer guests. Or, if you are using frozen raspberries, you will be able to serve it to guests all year round. The gorgeous color and texture (without gelatin) make it a dramatic showpiece.

If raspberries are too pricey, substitute strawberries. For that matter, substitute any fresh fruit you wish, but avoid acidic fruit. Papaya and kiwi would be splendid substitutes, too.

What soufflé recipe could be easier, even if it did originate at one of the prime New York restaurants?

3 cups raspberries*
  (makes 1¼ cups purée)
6 egg whites
⅓ cup honey or
  ¾ cup superfine sugar
2¼ cups whipping cream
1 oz. Framboise—raspberry
  liqueur (optional)

One 6-cup (1½-qt.) soufflé dish, collared

Serves 8

Wash raspberries gently in sieve under cool running water. Handle as little as possible. Let dry.

Warm unbeaten egg whites and honey or sugar in top of double boiler or in a bowl over hot water. Remove from heat. Beat with electric beater until stiff. In separate bowl, beat whipping cream.

In food processor bowl fitted with steel blade, place raspberries. Process quickly to purée. Be careful not to overprocess. If you are finicky about seeds, place raspberry purée in sieve, and with a wooden spoon, mash the raspberry purée through sieve into large bowl. Add Framboise liqueur, if you wish.

With rubber spatula, fold one-third beaten egg whites into raspberry purée. Fold in remaining egg whites. Gently fold in whipped cream. Pour into collared soufflé dish; with a knife, level the top of soufflé dish. Refrigerate. Reserve remaining soufflé.

When soufflé has congealed, scoop in remaining soufflé to fill collar of mold. Place in deep freeze. Freeze at least 6 hours. When serving, remove from freezer. Place in refrigerator about 2 to 4 hours to soften (exact time depends on how long it was left in freezer) and serve ice-cold, never at room temperature. Remove collar before serving.

*If using frozen raspberries, let thaw. Drain excess syrup. Use two 10-oz. packages to obtain comparable amount of purée (1¼ cups).

Irish Mist Soufflé

When you have a hankering to serve an Irish dish that kissed the Blarney stone, Irish Mist Soufflé is the perfect solution. Because it is a no-cook soufflé, Irish Mist Soufflé is suggested for summertime, but, of course, its impeccable flavor makes it special the year round.

4 eggs, separated
2½ Tablespoons honey,
warmed or 4 Tablespoons
superfine sugar
1 Tablespoon Irish Mist
liqueur
2 packages (2 Tablespoons)
unflavored gelatin
2 teaspoons lemon juice,
strained
1 Tablespoon boiling water

One 4-cup (1-qt.) souffle dish,
collared

Serves 6-8

In food processor bowl fitted with metal blade, put egg yolks and honey or sugar. Process until creamy. Add Irish Mist. Process until mixed.

In a measuring cup, scatter gelatin on top of lemon juice. Add boiling water to melt gelatin. Add melted gelatin mixture to egg yolk mixture in food processor bowl still fitted with steel blade, and process briefly to integrate. Pour mixture into another bowl.

Beat egg whites until stiff and glossy. With rubber spatula, fold one-third beaten egg whites into Irish Mist mixture. Gently fold in remaining egg whites. Pour into soufflé dish. Freeze at least 4 hours.

Remove from freezer 15 to 20 minutes before presenting and serve semi-frozen.

Superfan Chilled Orange Soufflé

Superfan Chilled Orange Soufflé is sensational! If you've ever been worried about your soufflé not rising, you'll have no problems whatsoever with this recipe. It ascends to celestial heights just as all Bronco Superfans do with a Bronco WIN!

2 egg yolks
1 cup superfine sugar or
¾ cup honey, warmed
2½ Tablespoons flour
⅛ teaspoon salt
5/6 cup milk, scalded
¼ teaspoon vanilla
2 Tablespoons orange zest,
grated
⅓ cup fresh orange juice
3 Tablespoons Grand Marnier
liqueur
5 egg whites at room
temperature
⅛ teaspoon cream of tartar
1½ cups heavy cream, whipped

GARNISH:
Orange segments, seeded,
thinly sliced
2 Tablespoons semi-sweet
chocolate, grated

One 6-cup soufflé dish,
collared

Serves 8

Beat egg yolks with ¼ cup sugar or ¼ cup honey until thick and lemony in color. Beat in flour and add salt. Gradually add hot scalded milk so mixture remains smooth. Heat mixture over low heat as you stir constantly while it thickens. Cook until the taste of raw flour disappears. Add vanilla. Cool and cover with a piece of waxed or plastic paper on top to prevent its forming a skin. Chill.

Combine grated orange zest and juice with Grand Marnier and fold into the chilled mixture with a rubber spatula.

Beat egg whites until frothy. Add cream of tartar. Continue to beat egg whites while adding remaining sugar or honey very gradually to make a meringue-like consistency. Beat until mixture forms shiny peaks.

Fold chilled orange mixture into meringue mixture. Gently fold in whipped cream and pour into prepared soufflé dish. Place in freezer overnight to firm.

Before serving, remove collar and allow soufflé to stand at room temperature for an hour. Decorate top with orange segments. Grate chocolate over top of soufflé to simulate browning.

The Egg, Etcetera

Chapter VII

Amazing Aspen Omelet

Ignite and send to table this sybaritic Aspen Omelet which a visiting cook made for us the weekend our group went to that town to view nature's perennial spectacle: the turning of the aspen foliage.

Whether you serve this in Aspen, Denver or wherever, Aspen Omelet makes any brunch a party and is easy to produce. You will quickly add it to your permanent recipe file.

3 medium cooking apples
2 teaspoons butter
1 Tablespoon Calvados
  apple liqueur or
  apple jack brandy
6 eggs
Additional 1 teaspoon butter

FOR THE GLAZE:
1½ teaspoons sugar
Additional 2 Tablespoons
  Calvados or apple jack
  brandy

Serves 4

Core, peel and cut up apples. In food processor bowl fitted with steel blade, place apples around blades. Process swiftly to chop apples. Be wary of overprocessing.

Melt 2 teaspoons butter in small skillet. When butter sizzles, start apples cooking—about 15 to 20 minutes—before you start the omelet. When apples are soft, add 1 Tablespoon Calvados.

Preheat broiler.

Beat eggs briefly—about 30 seconds—with a fork. Do not overbeat. Put additional 1 teaspoon butter into separate pan or skillet. When butter is melted and sizzling, add beaten eggs. Shake pan constantly and, from time to time, slide a spatula under edges of omelet to check that the liquid center cooks. When surface is set, not dry, add apple mixture. Fold omelet and remove to ovenproof glass plate or platter.

Sprinkle with sugar for glaze and put under hot broiler. Be vigilant, as omelet will brown instantly. Remove from broiler.

Warm additional 2 Tablespoons Calvados in small pan and pour over omelet. Ignite.

Croque-Monsieur
(Ham and Cheese Sandwich
Dipped in Egg Mixture)

Croque-Monsieur is a very famous sandwich in France and definitely one we should copy. The translation of the French verb "croquer" is to eat hastily something which makes a crunching noise. Everyone knows "monsieur" means mister, but every man, woman and child craves these sandwiches. What an apt description of Croque-Monsieur: a quickly prepared sandwich eaten on the run.

So often recipes have a tendency to become exotic and unnecessarily complicated, whereas Croque-Monsieur is a very hearty, easy to make in a hurry, sandwich, outrageously good for impromptu luncheons and suppers.

Don't forget, as a variation, to cut Croque-Monsieurs into small squares and serve hot as a hefty hors d'oeuvre to accompany pre-dinner drinks.

¼ cup cold milk
2 Tablespoons quick mixing
  instant flour
½ teaspoon baking powder
2 eggs
½ lb. grated imported Swiss
  cheese* (Gruyère or
  Emmenthal)
2 Tablespoons Kirsch cherry
  liqueur
⅛ teaspoon cayenne
Salt and pepper, freshly
  ground, to taste
8 slices French bread,
  preferably stale (⅓" thick)
2 Tablespoons butter, at
  room temperature
8 thin slices cooked ham,
  cut to fit slice of bread

One baking sheet, lightly
  buttered with additional
  1 Tablespoon butter

*Use grater or food processor to
grate cheese in an instant.

**To make 8 open-face
sandwiches**

Preheat broiler to medium.

Mix together milk, flour and baking powder. Whisk until there are no lumps. Add eggs, cheese, Kirsch and seasonings. Mix well.

Lightly spread slices of bread with butter. Place a slice of ham on top of each slice of bread. Cover each slice of ham completely with cheese mixture.

Place baking sheet under broiler until tops of sandwiches are very light brown (about 3 to 4 minutes). Serve at once very hot.

Denver Omelet in Pita Bread

How can a Denver cookbook be complete without mention of the ever popular Denver Omelet? So here's a new twist: pack each portion into the pocket of some Pita bread. With the flavor of a spicy omelet, you get the accompanying taste of comforting Pita bread.

6 slices bacon, fried crisp, drained (reserve bacon grease)
1 medium-size tomato, peeled, diced
1 green pepper, peeled, diced
12 eggs, beaten with
  4 Tablespoons ice water
2 Tablespoons chopped onion
Salt and pepper, freshly ground, to taste
8 pieces Pita bread, halved, warmed

Serves 8

Crumble fried bacon.

Heat omelet pan or skillet. Pour in enough reserved bacon grease to just coat bottom of pan. When sizzling, sauté tomato and green pepper until barely brown. Remove them from pan and reserve.

With pan still hot, over medium heat, pour additional bacon grease just to coat bottom of pan. Add beaten eggs. Let mixture set and do not stir for at least 30 seconds. Add crumbled bacon, tomato and green pepper mixture, onion, salt and pepper. Stir together, then continue to cook mixture undisturbed. When omelet is moist on top but has ceased being runny, with a metal spatula, fold over one side of omelet partway. Then, still using spatula, fold over other side of omelet just to cover other portion. Carefully lift omelet onto platter and cut into individual portions.

Take one-half piece Pita bread, and stuff omelet into it. Serve hot at once.

Dick's French Toast

Though Dick is not the principal resident chef at his ski home away from home, he loves to cook breakfast for all his weekend guests. This recipe, which he has perfected by trial and error, he is willing to share with us.

One 8-oz. bottle *pure* maple syrup
1 or 2 long baguettes of French bread
5 eggs
¾ cup half-and-half
1 teaspoon nutmeg (preferably freshly grated)
1 teaspoon cinnamon
Vegetable oil for frying
1 cup chopped nuts (optional)

One large skillet

Serves 8
2-3 slices per serving

Warm maple syrup by placing bottle in pan of just-boiling water over medium heat.

Slice bread into medium-thick slices. If slices are too thick, trim crusts. Otherwise, this is unnecessary.

In a bowl, beat eggs until barely mixed. Add half-and-half gradually. Season with nutmeg and cinnamon.

In large skillet, pour in vegetable oil until it fills about 1"-1½" in skillet, deep enough to deep-fry bread. Turn heat to high to heat oil.

Dip a slice of bread into egg mixture. When oil is sizzling, place prepared bread slice in skillet. Brown bread on both sides until crusty. Sprinkle on nuts while French toast is cooking. (A very neat trick is to turn French toast sprayed with nuts. Try it.) Remove browned French Toast from skillet to serve very hot. Season again with cinnamon and nutmeg, if you like. I like.

Guests may pour over as much warmed maple syrup as their consciences will allow.

Olympian Soufflé Pancakes

In Colorado, should these pancakes be renamed Mt. Elbert's instead of Olympian? This recipe has revolutionized making pancakes with the result that no longer does the diner feel a dull thump as each bite of pancake lands in his stomach. Rather, eating these light pancakes transports one to previously unknown gustatory heights.

1 cup plain yogurt
1 cup small curd cottage
  cheese
¾ cup unbleached flour
1 Tablespoon honey, warmed
  or 1 Tablespoons sugar
1 teaspoon vanilla
4 eggs, separated
Oil or butter to grease
  grill or skillet

FOR THE SYRUP:
Pure maple syrup,
  with brandy (optional)

Makes about 24
(Serve 3 on a plate)

In a large bowl, mix yogurt with cottage cheese. (Do not use food processor or blender.) Fold in flour carefully. Add honey or sugar, vanilla and egg yolks. Batter will be slightly lumpy.

Beat egg whites until soft peaks are formed. Fold one-third of beaten egg whites into yogurt mixture, and then gently fold in remaining egg whites.

To cook pancakes, heat greased grill or skillet until the point when a drop of water will sizzle. If using an electric skillet, temperature should be between 300° and 350°. Drop about one-third cup batter to form each pancake. When bubbles are on the periphery of the pancake, turn it over and cook on other side. Each pancake will rise like a little Olympian soufflé.

Serve pancakes with melted butter. Pass pure maple syrup, and if you need strength to face the day, lace maple syrup with a little brandy. (Some of us prefer to start the day on our own!)

If you don't have enough diners to use up all the batter, you may refrigerate it up to four days, to use later. But to achieve the very best of Olympian Soufflé Pancakes' truly perfect and light texture, make batter just before cooking pancakes.

You may wish to regrease grill or skillet before cooking each new batch of pancakes.

Oven Strawberry Pancakes with Strawberry Butter

Need I remind you that any other appropriate fruit may be substituted when strawberries are not available? Personally, I will hold out until the first strawberry peeks through its foliage in my garden, or until I can buy strawberries at market. I not only love their fresh taste in these pancakes, but also, ardently admire their color.

3 pints fresh strawberries
⅜ cup brown sugar or
   ¼ cup honey, barely warmed
4½ Tablespoons unbleached
   flour
½ teaspoon salt
1½ cups half-and-half
12 eggs
3 Tablespoons butter
¼ cup powdered sugar

Eight 5″-6″ individual
   baking dishes or one
   large round baking dish

Serves 8
Fills eight 5″-6″ individual
   dishes or makes one
   giant pancake

Preheat oven to 450°.

Wash and then hull strawberries. Slice them into halves. Place them in bowl. Add brown sugar or honey and toss gently to mix. Reserve.

Into food processor bowl fitted with plastic blade, put flour and salt. With motor running, through feed tube, pour half-and-half and eggs, one at a time. Process until batter is smooth, though thin. Remove to a separate bowl and gently fold in strawberries.

Place one teaspoon butter in each individual baking dish, or 3 Tablespoons butter in large baking dish. Place individual dishes on baking sheets or baking dish in oven to preheat about 3 minutes.

Remove dish(es) from oven. Pour in about ½ cup batter into each individual dish or pour all batter into baking dish. Return to oven for 15 minutes or until pancake(s) is puffed and brown around edges. Remove from oven and dust with powdered sugar.

Serve guests pancake(s) dusted with powdered sugar directly from individual dishes or large baking dish. Should you wish to gild the lily, pass a bowl of Strawberry Butter for each guest to spoon over pancake(s).

(Continued on next page)

Strawberry Butter

This is so sinfully rich that if you have the will power to skip it, do. Marvelous, too, though, on muffins and biscuits. Why be strong?

Additional 1 cup
  strawberries
8 oz. unsalted butter
Additional ⅛ teaspoon salt
Additional 2 teaspoons
  powdered sugar

Yield: almost 2 cups
Prepare and halve strawberries as in directions for "Oven Strawberry Pancakes".

Into food processor bowl fitted with plastic blade, place cut up butter around blades. Process until butter is creamy. With motor running, add salt and powdered sugar through feed tube. Process until mixed. Remove butter mixture to separate bowl. Gently fold in strawberries. Serve Strawberry Butter in sauceboat or small bowl.

Surprise Pancake

This hot-shot recipe is a perfect spur-of-the moment dish. Use it for brunches, or light suppers before or after a sporting event or concert, or for any impromptu gathering. In fact, such a sure-fire recipe can even be included in your planned-ahead menus.

Another bonanza: you almost always have the necessary ingredients on hand. Sensational is the word for this pancake! No wonder it is reputed to be the *New York Times'* most requested recipe.

If you need to serve more people, or more portions, make the recipe again. Do not try to double this recipe.

½ cup flour
½ cup milk
2 eggs, lightly beaten
Whole nutmeg (grate
  ⅛ teaspoon)
4 Tablespoons butter
2 Tablespoons powdered sugar
Juice of half lemon

FOR THE TOPPING:
Selection of fresh fruit
  or jelly or marmalade

Serves 2-4
Preheat oven to 475°.

Into food processor bowl fitted with plastic blade, place flour, milk and eggs. Process briefly to mix. Leave batter a little lumpy. With a nutmeg grater or small cheese grater, grate nutmeg onto top.

Melt butter in a 10"-12" skillet with heatproof handle or wrap handle in aluminum foil. Place skillet in oven. (Use pastry brush to thoroughly coat inside of skillet with butter.) When butter is very hot, remove skillet and pour in batter. Bake batter in oven 15 minutes, or until pancake is golden brown. Pancake will rise like a soufflé, but not as evenly.

Sprinkle pancake with powdered sugar and return it to oven briefly for sugar to melt. Sprinkle with lemon juice and serve topped with a selection of seasonal fruit or jelly or marmalade, or just as is.

Shushed Eggs

Pronounce "shushed" shoó-shd. But no matter how you say it, Shushed Eggs are glorious enough to make for holiday breakfasts or to impress hungry house guests.

This recipe was born in Coahoma, Mississippi and represents family Southern cooking at its peak. The success of this dish depends on the generous amount of butter, delicately browned, in which eggs are cooked. Shushed Eggs are enhanced by bacon or ham and other breakfast trimmings.

6 eggs
3 oz. butter
2 Tablespoons cream
Salt and pepper, freshly
ground, to taste

Serves 6
(Make twice when serving
more portions)

In an iron skillet over medium heat, or in an electric skillet set about 325°, melt butter until brown, never black.

In a bowl, beat eggs very briefly until just broken up. Add cream, salt and pepper. Pour into skillet. Turn down heat to low or 250° for electric skillet. Cook eggs, very slowly, until mushy and creamy. Do not stir. Remove skillet from heat or unplug.

Divide into desired portions and with a metal spatula and spoon, scoop up each portion to serve. Be sure to get the whole portion and do not let any egg stick to bottom of skillet.

Denver Dividends

Chapter VIII

Denver Dividends

Each Denverite could recite which Denver Dividend is most meaningful to him. For some, it might be having witnessed the change from a smaller, slower-paced, insular city to today's Denver. Our sprawled-out city today is one of the most thriving ones in America and is now called The Energy Capital of the World. No mean accomplishment.

As you work, live and cook in Denver, you cannot help but feel the vibes of a city on the move. Although there has been a healthy and tremendous input from those people new on the scene, Denver natives still love to hold the fort. This mixture of the old guard with the new transplants is a dynamic combination.

All of this means that when you live in Denver, you constantly will be amazed how many "old friends" and new ones, too, from all over the United States—even the world—can find you.

With this fact in mind, my Denver Dividends recipes have been divided by months into appropriate occasions so that you will quickly find a menu suitable for any time of year.

The dishes for each month constitute an outline of the menu. You can expand it easily or contract it as you see fit. Always add a fresh green or yellow vegetable, in season, cooked to just fork-tender. A starch or grain should also be an integral part of a dinner menu, and you will have rounded out your meals, nutritionally.

Feel free to use my recipes in all of the various chapters. Mix and match the dishes to your heart's content until you create the menu fitting your special occasion.

All starred items in menus that follow appear in *Denver Delicious*.

Menus for Year-Round Entertaining

January Dinner for Skiers
in Denver or at a Ski Resort
Hot Bloody Mary Soup*

Paella Valenciana*

Fresh Fruit

For kids to make after a snowfall: Maple Snow*

February Intimate Dinner for Lovers
Brie or Camembert Wafers*

Individual Beef Filets

Wild Rice Salad*

Very Lemon Bread with Lemon Pour*

Almond Bark Candy*

February Ground-Hog Day Dinner for Eight
Jerusalem Artichoke Soup*

Chinese Crystal Chicken with Broth*

Tabbouleh*

Pecan Moons*

March Dinner to Celebrate St. Patrick's Day

Wolfgang's Cucumber Soup*

Whole Stuffed Cabbage with Salsa de Jitomate
(Tomato Sauce)*

or

Vegetable Pâté*

Rosemary's Spoon Bread*

Irish Coffee Pudding*

or

Irish Coffee*

April Lenten Dinner
Spaghetti Trigère (first course)*

Simple Paella*

Cole Slaw with Staying Power*

Lemon Hot Cross Buns*

Fresh Fruit

FOR EASTER:

How to Dress Up A Ham*

Easter Bunny Dessert*

May Dinner for Mother's Day or
To Congratulate a Graduate

Relaxed Roast Beef with Yorkshire Pudding*

Cooked Cabbage Salad with Yogurt
and Caraway Seed Dressing*

Fudge Brownie Mortarboards*

or

Pineapple Extravaganza*

June Dinner For Father's Day or
For Visiting Parents of the Bride or Bridegroom

Shrimp Fluff*
(served with drinks)

Ginger Veal Tonnato*

Quick Herbed Onion Bread*

Tropical Bananas*

with

Brandy Snaps*

July Dinner to Whoop It Up for July Fourth

Hot Clam Consommé with Sherry*

or

Cold Curry Cream Soup*

Chinese Stir-Fried Chicken and Asparagus*
(substitute broccoli for asparagus)

Watermelon Balls with Raspberry Ice*

or

Strawberry Bonbons*

or

BOTH!

Labor Day Dinner for Weekend Guests

Trout in Red Wine Aspic*

Tomato Mousse* and Horseradish Mold*

Rosemary's Spoon Bread*

Plugged Melon*

or

Fresh Peach Ice Cream*

September Outdoor Farewell Dinner for Kids Returning to School
Or Summer's Last Fling

Cornhusk Trout Barbecued*

Wild Rice Salad*

Herring Salad*

Honeyed Beer Bread*

Microwave Chocolate Chip Cookies*

or

Tried-and-True Chocolate Chip Cookies*

Denver Surprise (Flowerpot Dessert)*

October Dinner for Parents of Trick-or-Treaters

Chilled Curried Zucchini Soup*

Ham à la Kirkpatrick*

Slimming Vegetables à la Grecque*

or

Tabbouleh*

Coffee Pumpkin Flan*

or

Bronco Outasight Cake*

November Dinner for Thanksgiving Week**

Israeli Avocado Soup* with
Almond Cheese Wafers*

How to Dress Up a Ham* with Beaten Biscuits*

Horseradish Mold* (cut down to size)

Cranberry-Juniper Berry Relish*

Green Salad with Gertrude's Sour Cream Dressing*

Pineapple Extravaganza*

**By changing the ham to a turkey, this could be an elegant Thanksgiving feast.

Denver Dividends

**December Christmas Week Dinner
For Just the Family and Close Friends**
Green Peppercorn Pâté*
Cal's Sukiyaki*
Green Salad with Mehlman Dressing*
or
Baked Cucumbers*
Artichoke Hearts Gratinées*
Snow Squares with Butter Sauce*
To Make for Christmas Gifts:
Almond Bark Candy*

December Dinner for the Family on Christmas Eve
Cold Curry Cream Soup*
Individual Beef Filets
Fettuccine Fling with Cold Tomato Sauce*
Green Salad
Your Favorite Soufflé Recipe (hot or iced)

**For Christmas, Trim-The-Tree Parties,
Open Houses and for Christmas Day**
Treasured Homemade Eggnog*
Brown Palace Macaroons*
Brandy Snaps*

To Cross Over into the New Year
Divinity*

Almond Cheese Wafers

These wafers beat store-bought ones hands down.

3½ oz. sharp cheddar cheese,
  shredded (should measure
  1 cup)
4 oz. butter
½ cup sliced almonds
1 egg, beaten (2 Tablespoons
  for dough, the remainder
  for glaze)
¾ cup all purpose flour,
  sifted
½ teaspoon baking powder
¼ teaspoon salt
¼ teaspoon chili powder
⅛ teaspoon dry mustard

One cookie sheet, ungreased

Makes about 25 crackers
Preheat oven to 350°.
Use shredder of food processor to grate cheese. Remove from bowl and reserve.

Change to steel blade in food processor and quickly process butter and almonds until well blended. Add 2 Tablespoons beaten egg and process until just incorporated.

Add flour, baking powder, salt and spices. Process until mixture is smooth. Add cheese and process until dough is mixed.

Roll into small balls and place on ungreased cookie sheet. Flatten wafers with a fork and brush tops with remainder of beaten egg.

Bake in upper section of oven 25 minutes or until edges of wafers are lightly browned. Cool on a wire rack. Store in tin.

Brie or Camembert Wafers

Perfect to accompany cocktails or juices. Make Brie or Camembert Wafers way ahead and hope they last.

8 oz. Brie or Camembert,
  ripe, brought to room
  temperature
3 oz. butter, softened
2 eggs
½ teaspoon salt
⅛ teaspoon pepper
Pinch cayenne
2 cups unbleached flour,
  sifted

GLAZE:
Additional 1 egg, beaten
  with 1 Tablespoon water

One cookie sheet, lightly
  greased

**Makes forty-eight to fifty
  1″ crackers**
Preheat oven to 350°.
Scrape crusts off of cheese, a nibbling bonus for a hardworking cook! Blend cheese with butter in food processor fitted with steel blade. Add eggs, salt, pepper and cayenne. Process quickly.

Slowly blend in flour and process until dough forms a soft ball.

Wrap dough in waxed paper and chill 30 to 60 minutes in refrigerator. Roll out dough on floured board until ¼″ to ½″ thick. Cut into small circles and place on cookie sheet. Brush each cracker with egg glaze and bake in upper third of oven 10 to 20 minutes, or until bottoms are slightly browned.

Roquefort Macadamia Balls

If Hawaii is your garden spot, bring back several jars of that state's macadamia nuts to keep on hand to make this recipe and to share with cooks like me. If Roquefort cheese is one of your favorite cheeses, you can already taste this sprightly combination in your imagination.

Should you be on an economy kick (who isn't?) substitute Danish Bleu Cheese for the Roquefort. Either way, these filling appetizers will light up the way for a special euphoric feeling.

3 oz. macadamia nuts
2 sprigs parsley, coarsely
  cut up
3 oz. Roquefort cheese,
  cut up
4 oz. unsalted butter,
  cut up
⅓ teaspoon paprika
⅛ teaspoon cayenne

Yield: Twenty ¾″ balls
(can double recipe, if desired)
Preheat oven to 350°.

Toast nuts by scattering them in one layer on baking sheet. Bake them about 8 minutes. Shake nuts once or twice during baking time. They should attain a golden brown color. Remove from oven and let cool.

Into food processor bowl fitted with steel blade, place parsley. Process to mince. Add toasted nuts. Process briefly with on-off pulse to finely chop, but not purée. Add Roquefort cheese and butter around blades. Process briefly to mix well. Add seasonings. Remove mixture. Refrigerate 30 minutes before making small balls from mixture. Refrigerate again.

Remove Macadamia Balls from refrigerator about ten minutes prior to serving time. Unnecessary to insert toothpicks into Macadamia Balls, as they should be quite firm.

Shrimp Fluff

Here is the perfect hors d'oeuvre and it takes only two minutes to prepare. It is so good your guests will think you were in the kitchen all day. Serving a hot hors d'oeuvre always bring compliments.

An accidental variation of this recipe at our house was a mixture of 4 oz. baby bay scallops (cut into fourths) with 4 oz. bay shrimp, instead of using all shrimp. If you share my passion for scallops, this variation will please you immeasurably.

8 oz. cooked bay shrimp
  (if only larger shrimp are
  available, cut into small
  bite-size pieces)
6 oz. cream cheese
⅛ teaspoon cayenne
¼ teaspoon white pepper
1 Tablespoon Worcestershire
  sauce or to taste

Serves 8
Pat shrimp dry with paper towels. In top of double boiler, place shrimp, cream cheese and seasonings. Correct seasonings, if necessary. Heat until all ingredients are thoroughly mixed. Serve warm with crackers or Melba toast.

Cold Curry Cream Soup

An instant soup that is spicy and extremely potable. Serve all year around. Chutney gives this soup umph.

2-3 cloves garlic
4 cups yogurt
4 cups chicken or beef
  stock (reserve ¼ cup)
2-3 teaspoons (depending on
  your taste) curry powder
  dissolved in ¼ cup reserved
  stock
2-3 Tablespoons chutney

GARNISH:
Chopped chives
Additional 1 Tablespoon
  chutney for each soup cup

Serves 8

Into food processor bowl fitted with steel blade and with motor running, drop garlic cloves. Process briefly to mince. With motor running, pour yogurt, stock and dissolved curry powder through feed tube. Process to mix. Add chutney. Process to mix. Or, use blender. Pour into separate bowl to refrigerate.

Serve in chilled soup cups or mugs and sprinkle each cup of soup with chives and chutney.

Denver
Dividends

Israeli Avocado Soup

Have you ever tasted a blah avocado soup and compared it with an avocado soup to dream about? This Israeli Avocado Soup recipe is, of course, one to relish and make frequently. A terrific way to start a meal. An eye-catching presentation is to serve it cold from half-cantaloupe shells. Or served hot, on a cold winter's night, it provides contentment for all who drink it.

4 Tablespoons butter
Five ½″ slices fresh
  ginger root, peeled
¼ cup unbleached flour
1½ cups milk
1 teaspoon grated lemon zest
3 large ripe avocados
1 Tablespoon fresh lemon juice
½ cup milk
½ teaspoon salt
3 cups half-and-half

GARNISH:
8 half-cantaloupe shells
6 small round cantaloupe
  balls for each soup cup,
Additional 1 Tablespoon
  fresh lemon juice
Additional 1 teaspoon (or more)
  finely grated ginger for
  each cup of soup

TO SERVE:

Serves 8

Melt butter in a medium-size pan over low to medium heat. Add ginger and cook slowly 10 minutes. Remove ginger from pan and discard. Whisk in flour, and cook 5 additional minutes as you stir constantly. Pour in milk gradually. Add lemon zest. Cook mixture over low heat 10 minutes or until mixture is smooth.

Peel avocados and remove seeds. In food processor fitted with steel blade, place cut up avocados. Spray on fresh lemon juice immediately to preserve color. With motor running, pour milk through feed tube. Add salt. Process briefly to mix.

Combine avocado mixture with white sauce. Add half-and-half.

Thoroughly chilled soup may be served cold in half-cantaloupe shells. Or, Israeli Avocado Soup may be heated slowly in the top of a double boiler and served hot. In either case, garnish with small round cantaloupe balls marinated in fresh lemon juice and additional finely grated ginger.

Jerusalem Artichoke Soup
with Italian Sauce

This soup with its novel and handsome presentation was conjured up by a British food expert, Glynn Christian, when he and I were "cooking up" together for a party luncheon in Denver at my house. Believe me, Glynn's smashing soup recipe will be around my kitchen for a long time to come, especially on a cold, blizzardy day, like the day he made it in Denver.

Glynn's Note: neither salt nor pepper is added at any stage in the cooking of this soup. Salt will come from the bacon in the tomato dressing. Black pepper (which could ruin the look of the basic soup) is added to the Italian Sauce just before serving, to preserve its aroma and to prevent its going bitter.

3 lbs. Jerusalem artichokes
2 Tablespoons cider vinegar or
  2 Tablespoons fresh lemon
  juice
1 cup chicken stock
1 quart milk or
  half-and-half
½ teaspoon mace

Serves 8

Scrub Jerusalem artichokes well. Place them in pan with boiling water to cover. Add vinegar or lemon juice. Boil Jerusalem artichokes, covered, about 15 minutes. If not fork-tender, continue to boil and test after 10 minutes. Do not cook too long, as overcooked Jerusalem artichokes quickly return to their tough native state. (Save ½ to ¾ cup water in which Jerusalem artichokes were cooked.)

Cool Jerusalem artichokes slightly. Using a vegetable peeler, skin them. A very tedious operation but it is simpler than peeling them before cooking when you care about the pure white color of the soup.

Into food processor bowl fitted with steel blade, place peeled Jerusalem artichokes with ½-¾ cup water in which they were cooked. Process to purée. Combine purée, chicken stock and milk or half-and-half. Remove mixture to medium-size pan and simmer gently about 30 minutes over low heat. Do not boil! Add additional chicken stock, if necessary, to attain medium-thick texture. Add mace. Keep mixture warm.

(continued on next page)

Italian Sauce

Make this unusual sauce while soup is simmering.

**4-6 slices bacon, cut into
½″-¾″ pieces
3 large tomatoes, peeled,
seeded and chopped
4-6 cloves garlic, minced
Pepper, freshly ground, to
taste**

**FOR SERVING:
GARNISH:
4 oz. whipping cream,
whipped
Several parsley sprigs, chopped**

Place bacon in small pan to sauté. When fat is running freely and bacon is starting to crisp, add tomatoes and garlic. Simmer mixture gently, uncovered, until it has mushed into a thick sauce. Add pepper just before serving. (See note at beginning of recipe.)

Pour Jerusalem Artichoke Soup into soup tureen or bowl. Into sauceboat or small bowl, pour Italian Sauce.

Scoop whipped cream into separate smaller bowl.

Pour soup into individual heated soup bowls. Using a spoon, make a well in center of thick soup and pour Italian Sauce into well. Garnish with a large dollop of whipped cream and add a sprinkling of chopped parsley on top for color.

Cal's Sukiyaki

Cal was one of the first American Marines to land in Japan after World War II. At that time, Japan was completely Eastern and scrupulously guarded all her customs, including her traditional recipes with traditional ways to serve them. Thus, Cal learned how to make Sukiyaki the true Japanese way.

Like many men chefs, Cal brought this recipe back to Denver in his head and, ever since, has delighted guests both with the flavor and presentation of his tempting recipe.

What differentiates Cal's recipe for Sukiyaki from the ordinary ones found in cookbooks is the poaching of individual eggs in the juices. In Japan, when serving Sukiyaki, the poached eggs are a separate course after the meat, vegetables and rice.

Dieters will cherish this recipe for a one-dish meal, as it is made without any oil whatsoever. Ingredients provide a bevy of vitamins and minerals, all so good for your body. The ease of preparation and the flourish of cooking it at table are boons to your soul. This recipe is a paragon for an evening meal either during a ski-weekend or served in your home.

1½ cups raw rice
(makes 6 cups cooked)
6 oz. sirloin strip, all
fat removed, partially
frozen
1 green pepper, membrane and
seeds removed
3 stalks celery, leaves
removed
1 large onion or 1 bunch
scallions with tops
½ lb. mushrooms, cleaned,
ends of stems removed
1 cup beef stock
¼ cup water
½ cup soy sauce
¼ cup dry sherry or
Japanese sake (optional)
4 oz. (from an 8-oz. can) water
chestnuts (optional)
¼ lb. spinach leaves, washed,
stemmed

Serves 8

Cook rice as per package directions. Keep warm.

To prepare ingredients: cut slightly frozen meat to fit feed tube of food processor. In its bowl fitted with slicer, place meat in feed tube. Process with medium pressure to slice. Reserve.

Cut green pepper to fit feed tube and process in same manner to slice. Place in separate bowl. Cut celery to fit feed tube and process to slice. Place celery in separate bowl. Cut onion to fit feed tube and process to slice. Place in separate bowl. Put mushrooms in feed tube and process to slice. Place in separate bowl.

(continued on next page)

TO ASSEMBLE AT TABLE:
8 eggs

One electric skillet

Have bowls prettily arranged with individual vegetables ready on a nearby tray. Pour beef stock and other liquids in skillet and heat at a-bout 325°. (If using a regular skillet, heat until just under a boil.) When stock is hot, cook green pepper first. One minute later, add celery. One minute later, add beef. One minute later, add onion. Add mushrooms and water chestnuts near the last. Adding fresh spinach leaves at the very last gives Sukiyaki a lovely fresh taste. This entire process of cooking Sukiyaki should take about six minutes, but beef should be well done, rather than rare.

Serve drained Sukiyaki hot on individual plates over hot rice. Reserve juices.

After everyone has finished eating his portion of Sukiyaki, and any second helpings have been served, reheat juices until they come to a boil to poach eggs.

To poach an egg: carefully break egg into a cup. Then, pour egg into hot juices. With a spoon, scoop up juices and spoon over top of egg. Egg should poach in about 3 minutes. This is the traditional way of serving Sukiyaki in Japan. Serve a poached egg to each guest.

Chinese Stir-Fried Chicken
and Asparagus

This recipe is a great example of why Chinese cuisine is inexpensive, chic and less caloric than most entrées. If you haven't yet attempted a Chinese dish, commence with this star.

Although these ingredients can be prepared a few hours prior to cooking time, this stir-fry technique has to be done at the last minute. The actual doing, however, is immense fun for your family or guests to watch.

**4 large chicken breasts,
halved, boned, skinned**
4 Tablespoons soy sauce
4 cloves garlic, minced
**40 fresh asparagus spears
(pencil-thin spears preferable)**
**2 green peppers (can use
red peppers, if in season)**
2 medium onions, peeled
**4 Tablespoons safflower or
peanut oil (possible additional
2 teaspoons)**
4 Tablespoons dry sherry
6 Tablespoons chicken stock

Wok or large skillet

Serves 8
Cut large chicken breasts into bite-sizes. Mix soy sauce with garlic. Add chicken. Let marinate at least 1 hour.

Wash asparagus spears thoroughly. Cut off tough bottom ends of stalks. If stalks are still tough, peel off any remaining tough parts of stems. Slice stalks into bite-sizes, diagonally, but leave tips whole.

Slice tops off peppers and remove membranes and seeds. Cut peppers into strips and then into bite-sizes. Cut onions into bite-sizes.

Heat wok or skillet with 2 Tablespoons of the oil. Swirl oil around to coat pan. Add marinated chicken and stir-fry (ideally use chopsticks) about 2-3 minutes, tossing until all chicken pieces turn white. Remove to platter or plate.

There should be enough oil left in the wok but, if necessary, add additional oil. Stir-fry peppers and onions. Remove and add to chicken. Add remaining 2 Tablespoons oil to wok. When sizzling, stir-fry asparagus about 2 to 3 minutes over high heat. Turn heat to low. Add sherry and chicken stock. Cover wok and simmer 3 minutes. Asparagus should be tender, yet crisp, and attain a bright green color. Return chicken with peppers and onions to wok. Stir briefly just until heated through. Serve hot at once.

**Denver
Dividends**

157

Ginger Veal Tonnato

Veal Tonnato, that sacred Italian dish of veal with a tuna fish sauce, is much enhanced when you have the courage to use my special touch: the addition of fresh ginger.

Although Veal Tonnato is considered a summer dish, don't forget about it in the dead of winter. Since the veal is cooked the day ahead, life becomes considerably easier for the host or hostess the day company is expected. Or, be a big spender and serve it to just the family as a very special treat.

3½-4 lbs. veal, cut from the leg, rolled and tied
1 large onion, unpeeled, chunked
2 stalks celery with leaves, chunked
1 carrot, unpeeled, chunked
3-4 Tablespoons any fresh herb (may use parsley)
½-1 cup dry white wine

One large Dutch oven or heavy kettle

THE FOLLOWING DAY:

FOR THE SAUCE:
1 cup Broadmoor's Ginger Dressing*
1 sour pickle, diced
One 7-oz. can tuna, water-packed, or oil removed, flaked
One 2-oz. can anchovies, oil removed, chopped
1 Tablespoon capers

Serves 8

Into Dutch oven or heavy kettle, place meat. Pour cold water into pan to cover. Bring water to boil. Lower heat and simmer about ten minutes. Remove pan from heat. Take veal out of pan; drain and wash veal thoroughly under cool running water. Also, rinse out pan completely.

Place veal back into clean pan. Add vegetables and herb. Generously cover with fresh water. Add wine. Bring to a boil. Reduce heat to simmer. Cover top of pan with a round of waxed paper and cover with lid. Simmer about 1½ hours or until meat can easily be pierced with a fork. Remove lid and waxed paper.

Refrigerate pan with meat and broth immediately, lest they sour. Do not cover pan until broth is cold.

Remove veal from broth. Wrap in foil and again refrigerate. Veal should be served very cold.

Place pan with broth over high heat. Bring to boil. Reduce broth to one cup. Allow to cool to lukewarm.

In a bowl with Broadmoor's Ginger Dressing, add pickle, tuna, anchovies and capers. Whisk in boiled-down lukewarm broth (about 1 cup) from veal. Pour mixture into bowl and refrigerate at once.

158

Ginger Veal Tonnato continued

TO SERVE:

Green Rice* is splendid with Ginger Veal Tonnato. When preparing a platter, make a bed of Green Rice. For individual plates, make a nest of Green Rice or put rice alongside two or three slices of veal. Veal should be sliced medium-thin. For the platter, place slices of veal, diagonally overlapping, over rice. Either cover veal with sauce or pass it in a sauce-boat separately. Follow same pattern for preparing individual plates.

Denver Dividends

*Recipe found in *Denver Delicious.*

Paella Valenciana

Whenever I volunteer to "cook up" for my family or friends while they are indulging in winter sports, this is the dish I always choose. Although the fish in my recipe is so expensive that you almost faint, compare its price with a restaurant check at a ski resort after you have hosted family or friends. That comparison will relieve your guilt. Also costly is the spice saffron. Why? Because it is made from the scarce stamens of the crocus flower. You can eliminate the saffron in the paella, but I do not advise it. Fortunately, you will need very little saffron.

Preparing and cooking Paella Valenciana is relatively easy, but takes a watchful eye during cooking. What frugal cook wants to see all that pricey fish overcooked and tough?

When presented with an asparagus garnish, Paella Valenciana is outrageously beautiful. When asparagus is not in season, make sure the pink lobster meat and shrimp, both cooked in their shells, with a scattering of clams and mussels in their shells are arranged attractively. The garnish should be mounded on top.

Years ago when I needed this recipe to take to Aspen and was in my customary last minute flurry to get ready to go, I asked Mother to write down the recipe from a very large cookbook. After three pages of notes, Mother wrote: "The End. Probably the end of the guests, too!"

Although the recipe is long, it is a one-dish meal. A very light dessert, such as fresh fruit, fruit ice or sherbet, should follow. A white wine, for instance, a white Burgundy, to drink completes what will be undoubtedly the most memorable meal you will serve or eat for a very long time to come. Also, remember it is unnecessary to stick to my ingredients verbatim. You can substitute what will please you and your purse.

2-3 uncooked medium-size lobster tails (reserve some shell for cooking)
18 Cherrystone clams
18 mussels
½ lb. (or more) crabmeat
¼ cup olive oil
4 whole chicken breasts, halved
¼ lb. veal
¼ lb. pork (Ask butcher to grind veal and pork together, or do it in food processor with steel blade. Do not overprocess.)
2-3 cloves garlic, minced
1-2 medium-size onions, finely chopped

1 teaspoon salt
¼ teaspoon pepper, freshly ground
2 medium-size tomatoes, seeded, chopped
2 cups raw rice
4 cups chicken stock (reserve ¼ cup)
1 green or red pepper, membrane and seeds removed, sliced into strips
1 package (10-oz.) frozen peas
1 package (10-oz.) frozen artichoke hearts
Additional clove of garlic, minced
⅛ teaspoon saffron

Serves 8

With heavy kitchen scissors, cut lobster tails into 1½" to 2" pieces. Some of the lobster shell (about one-fourth to one-third of the tails) should be reserved for cooking. Scrub clams and mussels. If sandy, place in a bowl of cool water to cover and add baking soda. You may have to repeat this process two or more times to release sand. Pick over crabmeat to discard any bone or tissue.

In skillet or shallow paella dish (mine is 13" in diameter) heat olive oil in pan over high heat. When sizzling, lower heat to medium and add chicken, veal and pork mixture. Cook until chicken is browned on

Paella Valenciana continued

both sides. Add garlic and onions and cook until soft. Season with salt and pepper. Add tomatoes. Cover skillet or dish and cook about 10 minutes. Stir in rice and chicken stock. Mix thoroughly to combine. Add pepper, peas and artichoke hearts. Cook over low heat about 30 minutes. Stir continually.

In a mortar, mash additional clove of garlic. Add to vegetables cooking. Mash saffron in mortar. Dissolve saffron threads in measuring cup with heated, reserved chicken stock. Add to paella in skillet. With a large spoon

GARNISH:
32 stalks medium-thin
   asparagus (about 20 stalks
   make 1 lb.)
1½ oz. pimiento, sliced
   into small strips
8 sprigs parsley

One exceptionally large skillet
   or large shallow paella dish

or metal spatula, check to see that rice does not stick to bottom of pan. Stir.

Add lobster and crabmeat. Cover pan and cook an additional 20 minutes or more. Be sure that lobster is thoroughly cooked.

In a separate deep pan, place clams and mussels with 2 cups water. Cover pan and bring to lively boil over high heat. Cook 5 to 7 minutes or until shells open. (Discard any clams or mussels with tightly closed shells. They are full of mud.)

Discard any tough stems of asparagus and peel rest of stalks, if necessary. Lay asparagus spears flat in a separate skillet with water to cover. Cover pan and boil about 8 minutes. Asparagus should be bitey and retain its original bright greenish color.

Be artistic in arranging the cooked paella. With a large spoon, scoop fish and rice mixture and place in paella dish. Decorate with pieces of lobster, mussels, clams and pimiento strips. Mound.

If using asparagus, place asparagus stalks over mound so that asparagus tips meet in center and stalks cover the paella. Garnish with parsley sprigs. Serve hot. When serving, give each guest a half chicken breast, some meat, some of every vegetable and fish. If any paella is left over, reheat the following day. The flavor will improve, if possible.

Anyone want to sign me up to prepare Paella Valenciana for a skiing weekend?

Relaxed Roast Beef
with Yorkshire Pudding

An absurdly easy recipe — heaven-sent for the benefit of busy careerists or housekeepers. Relaxed Roast Beef cooks all by itself, making the cook completely relaxed. This recipe cooks beef to a turn as well as being divinely simple.

When Yorkshire Pudding is cooked to perfection, it is the most. Cut it into squares and serve at table from the same dish in which it was cooked. In good old Yorkshire, this pudding was usually served as a separate course. But in good old Denver, it is an excellent accompaniment to roast beef.

4-rib prime standing roast at room temperature

Serves 8

Preheat oven to 500°.

Put roast into roasting pan. Do not salt roast as salt inhibits moistness. Bake 30 minutes. Turn oven off and do not peek.

Six to eight hours later (when you return from work or whatever) open oven door to get beef drippings for Yorkshire Pudding recipe. Close oven door quickly. Turn oven to 375°. Additional baking time begins only when oven reaches 375° temperature. Roast should bake additional 35-40 minutes. Use meat thermometer to discover exact internal temperature of roast. If you wish meat very rare, thermometer should register 140°—maybe even 120°—but if you like your beef medium, the thermometer should register 160°.

Remember to remove roaster from oven about 20 minutes before carving. Place meat on carving platter and let rest so meat will contract and carve more easily.

FOR THE YORKSHIRE PUDDING:
1½ cups unbleached flour
¼ teaspoon salt
⅛ teaspoon nutmeg, freshly ground
2 eggs
2 cups milk
¼ cup hot beef drippings

One oven-to-table square or oblong pan

Preheat oven to 400°.

Sift flour, salt and nutmeg into food processor bowl fitted with steel blade. Add eggs and process until mixed. With motor running, pour milk through feed tube. Process very briefly. (This much can be done ahead, but refrigerate batter.)
Into pan, pour hot beef drippings. Place pan in oven, and heat 10 minutes. Remove pan from oven and pour batter into pan. Batter should reach halfway up the sides of the pan. Bake 20 minutes. Reduce oven heat to 350° and bake an additional 10 to 15 minutes.

Simple Paella
(Chicken with Rice, etc.)

The word "paella" in Spanish means "pot". No matter which pot or skillet the cook uses, Paella will become a true friend.

Simple Paella is a modest dish without a lot of expensive fish and is an example of just good plain home cooking. A wise cook should always try to have a cooked Simple Paella available in his freezer, ready for drop-in guests.

½ cup olive oil
Two (2-lbs. each) chickens,
  cut up
1 teaspoon salt
½ teaspoon pepper,
  freshly ground
6 small onions or
  8 scallions with tops,
  chopped
2 cloves garlic, minced
2½ cups raw rice
1 cup dry white wine
3 cups chicken stock
1 Tablespoon fresh oregano
  or 1 teaspoon dried oregano
4 oz. almonds, slivered
½ cup stuffed olives,
  chopped
Additional 2 cups chicken
  stock

GARNISH:
18 medium-size
  mushrooms, quartered
2 Tablespoons butter

Serves 8

This paella may be cooked in the oven, but I prefer to cook it in a large skillet, or two medium-size ones, on top of the stove.

Heat olive oil in skillet(s) over high heat. (You can cut the olive oil down to ⅓ cup when using one skillet.) Place chicken pieces in skillet(s) to brown and lower heat to medium. Season with salt and pepper. Brown chicken on both sides. Add onions and cook about 15 minutes. Add garlic and rice and mix well. Pour in wine and chicken stock. Cover skillet. Cook at least 40 minutes. Taste to season.

Add oregano, almonds, olives and additional 2 cups chicken stock to make mixture moist. Keep covered over low heat to hold. This dish is even more flavorful the following day, reheated, as the flavors have had a chance to meld.

For the garnish, sauté mushrooms in butter. Sprinkle them decoratively on top of paella. Serve Simple Paella hot with a tossed green salad.

**Denver
Dividends**

163

Spaghetti Trigère

Rumor hath it that the famous dress designer, Pauline Trigère, created this recipe which I discovered abroad. Whoever invented it was a genius.

This is a most unusual first course and a great treatment of pasta without any cheese. For the main course at a supper, it is fantastic.

1 lb. thin spaghetti
3 Tablespoons butter
2 medium onions, chopped
1 lb. large mushrooms,
  sliced thick, or whole
  button mushrooms
⅔ cup whipping cream
1 Tablespoon (or more)
  nutmeg, freshly grated

Serves 8 as first course,
  4 to 5 as main course

Try to buy or make fresh pasta, but if that is not possible, always try to buy an Italian brand pasta.

Have large pan of salted water boiling, and gently stir in spaghetti. Cook just to the al dente (bitey) stage, only about 7-8 minutes.

In large sauté pan or skillet, melt butter over medium heat. Add chopped onions and sauté until soft. Add mushrooms. (You may wish to add an additional Tablespoon butter.) Add cooked spaghetti and whipping cream and mix. Serve immediately. Top with a generous amount of freshly grated nutmeg. The grated nutmeg makes it unique.

Trout in Red Wine Aspic

Aspic dishes are cold jellied dishes enfolding fish, poultry, meat, vegetables or fruit. Usually served in the summer, they are wonderful dishes for the host or hostess to include in a menu as they are always prepared well ahead.

Besides being unusually pretty and colorful, Trout in Red Wine Aspic is a very fast recipe to do. For a sweltering summer night, this dish is dynamite.

Gelatin must be treated carefully, lest you produce a rubbery concoction, unfit for anyone to eat. First, dissolve gelatin quickly in a glass measuring cup, with ¼ cup cold water. Stir to dissolve and use gelatin at once. Next, gelatin has to be melted. Either place measuring cup with gelatin in a pan of just-boiling water (bain-marie) to melt, or add dissolved gelatin to an already-cooked, but hot, mixture. When you follow religiously these two principles, you will never taste the gelatin.

4 whole trout, cleaned, skin left on
1 bottle of inexpensive red Burgundy or Pinot Chardonnay
2 packages (2 Tablespoons) unflavored gelatin dissolved in ¼ cup cold water
1 medium-size cucumber
1 bunch radishes
8 leaves of fresh herbs (except mint) such as tarragon, sorrel or sage

One large rectangular shallow dish or platter (large enough to lay four trout flat)

Serves 4
(May be doubled, but an extremely large dish or tray is needed for 8 trout.)

In large fish poacher or kettle, over medium heat, gently place whole trout. Cover with red wine. When wine comes to a boil, lower heat to simmer. Cook only 15 minutes. Add dissolved gelatin at the end of the cooking time. Heat just long enough to melt gelatin.

Remove trout and lay flat side-by-side on dish or platter. Reduce wine by rapid boil to about 2½ cups. Remove from heat and let stand 5 minutes. Pour over trout on dish or platter. Refrigerate.

If cucumber is waxed, scrub to remove wax but do not peel. Run fork tines up and down cucumber to make decorative ridges. Slice cucumber very, very thin. Wash and stem radishes. Discard leaves. Slice radishes thin.

Make design of alternating cucumber and radishes around edges of trout. Decoration should be flat. Place two herb leaves on each trout. Spoon a little red wine aspic over herb leaves and tops of trout. Refrigerate overnight or at least 4 hours.

Serve cold from same dish. Using a metal spatula, scoop under each trout gently to place on individual dinner plates. With a spoon, scoop up some red aspic with cucumber and radish slices to serve with each trout.

Whole Stuffed Cabbage
with Salsa de Jitomate
(Tomato Sauce)

This is a perfect entrée to cook up at one of the ski resorts, and though some might consider it food for peasants, let me be the first peasant to have it simmering ready to eat after a work-out on the slopes or after a brisk walk in newly fallen snow.

With French bread, a jug of simple red wine, followed by a cheese and fruit course, this is your whole meal. You will stun your family and guests with your originality.

**1 medium-to-large
  green cabbage**

Serves 4-6

There are two ways to treat cabbage for this recipe. If you have enough time, put tightly-wrapped cabbage into freezer, and leave overnight. Do not leave more than two days. Or, if you have limited time, drop cabbage into Dutch oven with already-briskly boiling water. Let simmer about 25 minutes, but watch so that cabbage does not overcook to become limp.

If the cabbage was in deep freezer, place cabbage briefly in a large bowl of very hot water for just enough time (3 to 5 minutes) that outer leaves will peel back easily. Do not attempt to defrost cabbage completely. If cabbage has been parboiled, remove from boiling water, and when cool, peel back several outer layers of leaves.

Whole Stuffed Cabbage with Salsa de Jitomate continued

FOR THE STUFFING:
**1¼ lbs. lean ground beef
or use top round,
completely defatted and
boned in food processor
with steel blade. While
motor is running, drop
small hunks of meat
through feed tube and
process quickly until meat
is a mass. Be wary of
overprocessing.
1 large onion, finely
chopped
2 cloves garlic, minced
1 medium tomato, peeled,
chopped
2 apples, peeled, cored
and chopped
1 fresh hot green pepper,
or 2 to 3 canned
Jalapeno chilies,
seeded and chopped
½ cup raisins, soaked
and plumped 10 minutes
in hot water
1 teaspoon oregano
1 teaspoon thyme
2 cans beef stock**

Cheesecloth

Mix all ingredients together, except beef stock. (It is not necessary to cook them prior to stuffing.)

After peeling back several of outer leaves of the cabbage, pile stuffing into center of cabbage. If your indentation is not large enough, with a knife, cut out a circle deep enough to encase stuffing. Put leaves back into original shape.

Place cheesecloth underneath cabbage and carefully fold up over cabbage so that every part is covered. With the folds, make a knot or two on top to tie everything together.

Into a Dutch oven or large pan, place cheesecloth-wrapped cabbage. Pour in beef stock and cover Dutch oven. Bring to a boil; reduce heat. Simmer cabbage 2½ to 3 hours.

Lift cabbage out with two large spoons. Drain and place on a round serving dish or platter. Untie and slide out cheesecloth. Lift the cabbage with a spatula to do this. Spoon a little Tomato Sauce over the cabbage and serve the rest of sauce in a sauce boat.

Reserve beef stock for tomorrow's hot soupe du jour.

To serve, cut cabbage into wedges. Accompany with rice.

(continued on next page)

**Denver
Dividends**

167

Tomato Sauce

For a recipe for a low-triglyceride sauce, skip the oil and simply spray skillet with a cholesterol-free oil. Wipe out excess oil with paper towels. Add tomato purée and follow rest of recipe.

Either way, Tomato Sauce incorporates some exciting tastes, and can be used equally well over your choice of pasta.

Additional medium-size onion, chopped
Additional clove garlic, minced
Additional 2 medium-size tomatoes, chopped (unnecessary to peel when using a food processor)
2 canned jalapeno chilies, chopped
4 teaspoons safflower or olive oil (or cholesterol-free oil)
1 Tablespoon fresh coriander, chopped, or 2 teaspoons dried coriander

Yield: approximately one cup

Combine all ingredients except oil and coriander and process in food processor or mix in blender. Purée briefly, as the purée should retain some texture, rather than being smooth.

Heat oil in skillet. When sizzling, pour in tomato purée. Cook over moderate heat, as you stir constantly, until mixture is thick and well blended—about 10 to 15 minutes. Stir in coriander.

Green Rice

Serving Green Rice is a spirited way to perk up jaded appetites. It beautifully solves the problem of which grain to serve for dinner. The addition of a fresh vegetable takes rice out of the doldrums.

2 cups long grain rice
½ lb. fresh spinach,
  washed, stems removed,
  chopped (use food
  processor with steel
  blade)
½ cup available fresh herbs
  (parsley, chives and tarragon)
Salt and pepper, freshly
  ground, to taste

Serves 8
Cook rice according to package directions. About 5 minutes before water has evaporated, add chopped spinach, fresh herbs and seasonings. Re-cover pan to let mixture steam. Remove from stove quickly. Fluff and serve hot.

Denver
Dividends

Horseradish Mold

This Horseradish Mold is a striking accompaniment to a whole ham, a whole turkey or a filet of beef, presented on a large buffet table. Its zippy taste is an enticing contrast to any meat or fish.

1 package (1 Tablespoon)
  unflavored gelatin
¼ cup chicken stock
1 small onion, grated
¾ cup horseradish
  (if root unavailable, use
  horseradish sauce, not
  creamed)
1½ cups sour cream
2 egg whites
½ teaspoon salt

One 4 cup (1-qt.) mold

Serves 30 or more
Yield: one quart (divide by
  half to make one pint)
Dissolve gelatin in chicken stock in glass measuring cup. Place cup in a pan of just boiling water to melt gelatin. Let it cool briefly. Combine onion, horseradish and sour cream with gelatin. Mix thoroughly.

Beat egg whites. When just peaked, add salt. Continue to beat egg whites until very stiff. Fold them carefully into horseradish mixture. Rinse mold in iced cold water. Pour off excess water but do not dry. Pour horseradish mixture into mold. Refrigerate.

Before serving, unmold by running a knife around edge of mold, then dipping mold into very hot water very briefly—about 5 seconds. If necessary, repeat. Reverse mold and give it a knock to unmold on a round platter or plate. Keep refrigerated until ready to serve.

Juniper Berry Cranberry Sauce

Instead of common canned cranberry sauce, and for a novelty, serve Juniper Berry Cranberry Sauce, warm or cold, with your holiday bird. Also to doll up the bird, copy our family tradition of making a cranberry necklace—just like stringing beads, so children can make it all by themselves.

Free juniper berries are found, of course, on juniper trees. Where else? But avoid green berries and wait until a frost turns them blue.

Besides being different, this Juniper Berry Cranberry Sauce boasts a ravishing carmine hue.

Zest of one orange
35 juniper berries
1 lb. cranberries
2 Tablespoons molasses
6 Tablespoons honey,
  warmed

Makes 2 cups

In food processor bowl* fitted with steel blade, place cut up zest around blades. Process until minced. Add juniper berries and process them until crushed.

In pan over medium heat, place juniper berry mixture, cranberries and molasses. Cook 8 to 10 minutes until cranberries pop and mixture begins to thicken.

Return cooked berry mixture to bowl of food processor, still fitted with steel blade. Whiz until desired texture is achieved (should be chunky). Add warmed honey and process until just mixed. If too tart, add additional warmed honey.

*An alternate method is to use a food mill and grind away. Takes elbow grease, however.

Asparagus Mousse

What vegetable can compete with asparagus as a harbinger of spring? Centuries ago, even the Romans knew to cook it quickly. When asparagus is laid flat in a skillet, and cooked only about 8 minutes after it reaches a boil, its pristine color will be preserved. It will bear no resemblance to that limp, soggy vegetable with which we are all only too familiar.

After you have mastered the technique of serving asparagus whole and properly cooked, try making a novel Asparagus Mousse. This dish doubles as the vegetable and the salad. The essence of asparagus, the fresh green color and the suavity of this mousse are bound to please the cook and all guests.

12 oz. fresh asparagus, tough ends removed, cut diagonally into 1"-1½" pieces
1 teaspoon vegetable oil
1 teaspoon salt
2 teaspoons butter
2 scallions with green tops, coarsely chopped
2 cloves garlic, halved
1 Tablespoon mixture of available fresh herbs (tarragon, thyme, rosemary) or 1 teaspoon mixed dried herbs
1 package (1 Tablespoon) unflavored gelatin
¼ cup cold water
⅔ cup whipping cream

One 4 cup (1-qt.) mold

Serves 8

Into pan of rapidly boiling water, plunge prepared asparagus. Add oil and salt to preserve color. Let boil briefly until asparagus pieces are soft (10 to 15 minutes after a boil has been reached). Drain asparagus immediately and reserve.

In small pan over medium heat, melt butter. When sizzling, add scallions and garlic. Cook until just softened.

Into food processor bowl fitted with steel blade, put drained asparagus, scallions, garlic and herbs. Process to purée. Let mixture rest until it is cool, not warm (may take 30 minutes).

Just before assembling, prepare gelatin and whip cream. Stir to dissolve gelatin in cold water. Place the cup in pan with hot water, over medium heat. The size of pan should be just a little larger than cup. Stir until gelatin melts.

To whip cream to attain maximum volume and best texture: pour cream into a small bowl. Place it in a larger bowl filled with at least 1 cup ice cubes. Commence by whipping cream at slowest speed of hand-held electric beater as you rotate small bowl. Increase speed until cream is stiff. When the cream is whipped perfectly, you can see the bottom of the bowl.

Fold whipped cream into asparagus mixture. Add prepared gelatin. Rinse mold with cold water. Pour out excess water but do not dry. Pour in asparagus mixture. Refrigerate at least four hours until firm.

(continued on next page)

To unmold: run knife around edge of Asparagus Mousse in mold. Dip bottom of mold very briefly, about 5 seconds, into a pan or sink of hot water. Reverse mold and give a strong whack.

Unmold on small plate or platter. Refrigerate at once. Remove from refrigerator to serve immediately.

Broadmoor's Ginger Dressing

As the leading resort in Colorado, the Broadmoor Hotel of international fame is a mecca for all who wish to take a brief holiday or are lured there to attend a convention. When Coloradoans are not there, they are dreaming about it. With a choice among its five dining rooms, one can be always well assured of a superlative meal, with a wine list that is the envy of all.

Ginger Dressing is a Broadmoor specialty and is especially adaptable for cold seafood. It could also be used admirably to dress a green salad.

1 egg at room temperature
2 teaspoons fresh lemon juice
½ teaspoon salt
¼ teaspoon curry powder
¼ teaspoon white pepper
½ cup olive oil
½ cup safflower oil
Ten ⅛″ slivers ginger
  (from ginger root) peeled

Makes one cup

Into food processor bowl fitted with steel blade, place egg, lemon juice, salt, curry powder and white pepper. Use on-off pulse about two times to blend. With motor running, pour combination of olive and safflower oils slowly through feed tube. When oils emulsify to thicken, add ginger slivers. Process until mixture is thoroughly blended.

Variation: To make plain mayonnaise quickly, use same procedure, but delete the curry powder and ginger and add, instead, 1 teaspoon Dijoy-type mustard. Spoon into jar with tight-fitting lid and refrigerate. Mayonnaise should keep for two weeks.

Cole Slaw with Staying Power

Have you ever yearned for a cole slaw recipe that has staying power and would not sour too quickly? Here is a recipe that is classy although made with ordinary ingredients which, thanks to the food processor, can be speedily combined to make an extraordinary salad.

For career persons who must be master menu planners, this do-ahead recipe is a godsend, because the taste improves over the week or more that Cole Slaw with Staying Power can last.

FOR THE SLAW:
1 head cabbage, quartered, chunked
2 stalks celery, leaves removed, chunked
½ zucchini, peeled, chunked
⅓ sweet red pepper, membrane and seeds removed, chunked
⅓ green pepper, membrane and seeds removed, chunked
One leek, cleaned, white bulb only

FOR THE DRESSING:
½ cup and additional 1 Tablespoon honey
¾ cup cider or white wine vinegar
1 cup safflower oil
1 teaspoon dried tarragon or 1 Tablespoon fresh tarragon
1 teaspoon chervil
1 teaspoon Dijon-like mustard
Pepper, freshly ground, to taste

TO SERVE:

Serves 8-10

Into food processor fitted with steel blade, place chunked cabbage and celery around blades. Process to chop coarsely. Add zucchini, red and green peppers and leek to bowl and process to chop coarsely. Remove vegetable medley to large salad bowl.

Combine ingredients and place in pan over high-medium heat to come to a boil, as you stir.

Immediately pour hot dressing over vegetables in salad bowl. Toss well. Cover bowl and refrigerate at least one day before serving.

Scoop with slotted spoon to drain liquid. Slaw will stay crisp and remain fresh, marinating in dressing, for at least a week.

Herring Salad

Out of respect for Denverites proud of a Scandinavian heritage, here is a notable Herring Salad. This recipe can be copied and made in jiffy time by Denver cooks today.

Herring Salad is very filling and, therefore, should be served as the main dish with little else to accompany it. If you are having a buffet party with several salads, be sure to include it, as it is both tasty and has a great deal of eye appeal.

12 oz. herring (not packed in cream)

2 medium-size cooked beets, julienned

¼-½ cucumber (depending on size of cucumber) peeled*, sliced very thin

1 Tablespoon dill pickle, diced

1-2 medium-size onions, thinly sliced into rings

2 Tablespoons yogurt (or sour cream)

HINT: When peeling cucumber, always peel from stem to blossom end so cucumber will have less acidity. This is what makes you burp.

Serves 8

If using canned beets, it is very important to place them in a sieve to wash off the additives under cool running water. Otherwise beets will "bleed", and the color will run into the salad.

In a salad bowl, mix herring with other ingredients. Add yogurt or sour cream to bind. Toss gently and swiftly. Place salad bowl, covered tightly with plastic wrap, in refrigerator. Chill at least 2 to 4 hours before serving.

Tomato Mousse

If you aspire to be a host or hostess with panache, serve a mousse. Tomato Mousse fits the bill admirably; it is easy to prepare and should be made ahead. Its deep rosy glow will enhance its sublime velvety taste.

2 Tablespoons unsalted
  butter
4 ripe tomatoes, peeled,
  coarsely chopped
2½ Tablespoons tomato
  paste or purée
⅛ teaspoon sugar
1 clove garlic
1 Tablespoon fresh thyme
  or 1 teaspoon dried thyme
1 Tablespoon chervil or
  1 teaspoon dried chervil
1 package (1 Tablespoon)
  unflavored gelatin: first
  dissolve in ¼ cup
  cold water, then place
  cup in a pan of just-
  boiling water to
  melt
½ cup whipping cream

One 4 cup (1-qt.) mold

GARNISH:
Chopped green chives
  (optional)

Serves 8

Melt butter in pan over medium heat. Add chopped tomatoes, tomato paste and sugar. Simmer until liquid evaporates.

Into food processor fitted with steel blade, place garlic and herbs. Process to mince. Add to tomato mixture. Simmer an additional 5 minutes. Let mixture cool 5 minutes. Pour tomato mixture into food processor bowl, still fitted with steel blade.

Process to purée. Remove to separate bowl. It is very important to let mixture now cool for an additional 30 minutes. Add melted gelatin and mix thoroughly.

Whip cream until stiff. Fold into tomato mixture to thicken it.

Rinse mold with iced cold water. Pour off excess water but do not dry. Pour in tomato mixture. Refrigerate until firm.

To unmold: Run knife around edge of tomato mousse in mold. Dip bottom of mold very briefly, about 5 seconds, into a pan or sink of hot water. Reverse mold and give it a strong swat. Tomato Mousse should unmold, without melting, on a small plate or platter. Refrigerate at once until serving time.

Before serving, if you wish, for a color and taste contrast, sprinkle top of mold with chopped chives.

Denver
Dividends

Lemon Hot Cross Buns

Do you remember the Mother Goose rhyme that goes "One a penny, two a penny, hot cross buns—If you have no daughters, give them to your sons"? Lemon Hot Cross Buns are most apropos for Lent, as well as "in" for an Easter brunch. You will find that the contrast of the sweet and sour tastes gives them a sublime flavor.

¾ cup lemon juice, hot
4 oz. butter, softened
¼ cup and additional
  1 Tablespoon honey,
  warmed
1 teaspoon cinnamon
½ teaspoon salt
2 packages (½ oz.) dry
  yeast
Additional ½ cup
  lemon juice, warmed
3 eggs
4 cups unbleached flour
1 cup golden raisins
1 Tablespoon lemon
  zest, grated

Two cookie sheets, greased

FOR THE GLAZE:
1 cup powdered sugar
1 Tablespoon boiling water

Makes 18

In a large bowl, pour hot lemon juice over softened butter mixed with warmed honey, cinnamon and salt. Cool mixture to lukewarm.

Dissolve dry yeast in additional warm (not hot) ½ cup lemon juice and cool. Add eggs to honey-butter mixture. Incorporate dissolved yeast mixture into honey-butter mixture and mix thoroughly. Add flour to make soft dough. Either in a mixer with dough hook attachment or with your hands on a floured board, knead dough until smooth. Add raisins and grated lemon zest. Place dough in a large greased bowl. Cover with a damp tea towel and let mixture rise in warm place until doubled in bulk (2 hours or more).

Punch dough down and turn out onto a floured board. Shape dough into 18 round balls and place them on baking sheets. Cover with damp tea towels, and let rise in warm place until doubled in bulk (2 hours).

Preheat oven to 350°.

With razor blade, cut a cross in the top of each bun. Bake about 20 minutes, rotating baking sheets after 10 minutes to ensure even cooking. Remove baking sheets from oven and let buns cool down to room temperature.

In a small mixing bowl, mix powdered sugar with boiling water. Drizzle glaze over each lemon bun.

Rosemary's Spoon Bread

Contrary to much foolish assumption, Spoon Bread is not and never has been a bread. Cookbook authors continue to ignore this fact and usually classify it with the breads. Rather, it is a first cousin once removed from a soufflé. Don't expect it to puff up as much as does its cousin.

Spoon Bread, a Southern heirloom, originates from an Indian porridge called "suppawn". Like all good things to eat, Spoon Bread has been adopted by countless Denver cousins (this recipe is a three-generation one), as it is a matchless accompaniment for any entrée. It is particularly tasty when it is napped with a fresh mushroom or tomato sauce.

Spoon Bread can be a fine carrier for any creamed dish, like leftover fish, poultry or a mixture of vegetables. Use what you have.

3 cups milk
⅔ cup cornmeal
1 teaspoon salt
1 Tablespoon sugar
3 oz. butter
3 egg yolks, beaten
4 egg whites

One 6-cup (1½-qt.) casserole
or soufflé dish, buttered

Serves 8-10

Preheat oven to 350°

Heat milk to a boil. Slowly stir in cornmeal, salt and sugar. Cook at least 5 minutes or until thick. Add butter while mixture is cooking.

Cool mixture to warm. Add beaten egg yolks. Beat egg whites until stiff, not dry. With a rubber spatula, gently fold in one-third of beaten egg whites. Then, quickly fold in remaining egg whites.

Pour batter into prepared casserole or soufflé dish. Bake about 40 minutes or until a straw inserted in center of dish comes out clean. Crust will be brownish and will puff somewhat. Serve immediately from the same dish.

Souffléed Crackers

I discovered this recipe long ago during World War II days when I was following the navy in general, and my husband in particular, around the country. At a recent splashy nuptial dinner, Souffléed Crackers surfaced to accompany the soup course. Every guest thought them unfathomable, though they are easy and simple to make. Incidentally, Souffléed Crackers, served piping hot or cold, are sublime with pre-dinner cocktails or juices.

8 squares of elongated crackers (sodium-free crackers work well)
Iced water
About 3 Tablespoons butter

One long deep pan for soaking
One teflon or oiled cookie sheet

Serves 8
(Serve at least 4 to each person)

Preheat oven to 450°.

Prepare cold water with ice cubes in deep pan. Break square into 4 separate crackers. Place in deep pan to soak 8 minutes. Crackers have a tendency to float, so poke them down from time to time so that every cracker is submerged and saturated.

With a spatula or your fingers, carefully scoop up each cracker and place on cookie sheet. Dot each cracker with about ½ teaspoon butter. Place cookie sheet in oven. Bake 13 to 15 minutes, or until crackers are crisp, souffléed and a light brown. Remove from oven immediately.

Bronco Outasight Cake
(alias Carrot Cake Iced)

Try this superb Bronco Outasight Cake on the home front while watching the Broncos on the tube. When hosting Bronco Buffets after returning from the stadium, this cake also is a crowd-pleaser.

Just like our Broncos, this cake has no rivals in its field. (So Denverites think.) And just as our Broncos steal touch-downs, I stole this recipe from my friend, Jaynn.

FOR THE CAKE:
2 cups and 2 additional
  Tablespoons cake flour
1½ Tablespoons cinnamon
2 teaspoons soda
1⅓ cups salad oil
  (not olive oil)
1 cup and additional
  2 Tablespoons honey,
  warmed, or 2 cups
  superfine sugar
4 eggs
2 cups grated carrots
1 cup pecans, chopped

One bundt pan, greased
  and heavily floured

FOR THE ICING:
1 large 8-oz. and
  additional 1 small 3-oz.
  bar of cream cheese
¼ cup unsalted butter
2½ cups sifted powdered
  sugar
1 Tablespoon vanilla

Serves 12-16

Preheat oven to 325°.

Sift flour. Add cinnamon and soda. Into food processor bowl fitted with steel blade, put flour mixture. With motor running, pour salad oil and honey or sugar through feed tube. Add eggs, one at a time, through feed tube. After each addition, process to mix. Remove to separate bowl. Add carrots and pecans to batter.

Pour into prepared bundt pan. Bake one hour and fifteen minutes.

Cool about 20 minutes before turning out on cake rack.

Have cream cheese and butter at room temperature. Cream together well. (Food processor fitted with steel blade does this quickly.) Add sugar and vanilla. Mix well.

Spread cream cheese icing on top and sides of cake with a metal spatula. To make icing more smooth, dip spatula into hot water.

Denver Surprise (Flowerpot Dessert)

My flowerpot dessert has been my most famous recipe over the years because of its adaptability. Originally, I served it in Denver with individual stems of rose buds decorating each dessert. Some of my most successful substitutes include everything from sunflowers (picked in vacant lots) to a bride and groom figure on a pipe cleaner. So let your own imagination soar.

Several years ago when it was our turn to entertain friends in Denver's sister city, Brest, France, I chose this dessert. Picture me trying to explain it in French!

The night of our dinner, when written menus were at each person's place, I glanced down at what was inscribed for the dessert. I saw "Denver Surprise" written. Along with our French guests, I anticipated the presentation of the dessert. I shall not keep you in suspense - it was one giant-size flowerpot, filled with homemade vanilla ice cream mixed with wild strawberries from Plougastel, next door to Brest. One top of this delicate dessert was a bouquet of Colorado carnations. This one time the hostess was as surprised as the guests.

The only caution to remember when making "Denver Surprise" is to cover the hole at the bottom of the flowerpot with a piece of pound cake, angelfood cake or any stale cake you have hanging around your kitchen. If you have none, go out and buy a plain angelfood cake.

Think of this Denver Surprise as individual Baked Alaskas. You will realize that we have come full circle from the day of Molly Brown's sumptuous dinner menu culminating in Baked Alaska Flambé.

Whenever you are planning a dinner for 25 or more guests, this is the perfect dessert, as the flowerpots filled with cake and ice cream can be prepared ahead of time and placed in your deep freeze (or a restaurant's or club's) ready for the meringue treatment, etc.

8 individual small clay flower pots (opening is 3⅛″ in diameter)
Pound cake or plain angelfood cake
1½ qts. (3-pts.) your favorite ice cream, slightly softened
Fresh fruit in season (optional)

Serves 8

Sterilize flowerpots. Simply place them upside-down in dishwasher and run full cycle without adding detergent. Cool flowerpots.

Break off pieces of pound cake or angelfood cake. Place a piece just large enough to fit bottom of each flowerpot to cover opening so ice cream will not leak out. Spoon ice cream or mixture of ice cream with fresh fruit over top of cake to fill three-fourths of each flowerpot. Place prepared flowerpots in freezer.

FOR THE MERINGUE:
6-8 extra large egg whites
½ cup superfine sugar

One shallow broiler pan

Preheat broiler to low.

Beat egg whites until barely stiff and glossy. Add sugar one teaspoon at a time. Meringue should be very stiff.

With a tablespoon, completely cover ice cream with meringue to seal in ice cream. Mound meringue over top of each flowerpot. Place flowerpots on broiler pan.

Broil under low heat about 3 to 4 minutes. Do not take your eyes off flowerpots while they are under the broiler! Meringue should be golden, not browned.

Remove flowerpots from oven. Serve each individual flowerpot dessert on a dessert-size plate. Place flower or decoration in center of each pot. Flower should be washed, but dry. Serve at once to awed guests.

Easter Bunny

When asked to dream up the menu for a ladies' spring luncheon event, I chose this dessert. As several hundred bunnies were placed on the tables for dessert, there was a rousing cheer from the crowd.

This no-cook dessert is so easy your children can help prepare it, and it is so tasty it will appeal to the child in every one of us! Happy Easter! Or just pretend it's Easter and serve it anyway.

1 quart vanilla ice cream
7 oz. shredded coconut
Candy-coated almonds or jelly beans
8 red maraschino cherries
Discarded ribbon or 1 cup whipping cream, whipped (optional)
2 medium bananas, peeled

Serves 6-8

Using an ice cream scoop, make six to eight individual balls of vanilla ice cream. Roll each ice cream ball in shredded coconut. This is the bunny's head. Make eyes with almonds or jelly beans and a nose with a maraschino cherry. (Wash cherries in a sieve under cool running water to rinse off red food coloring.)

For the bunny's necktie, either tie a bow of ribbon under his chin or, with a pastry bag, make a whipped cream collar around his neck. Fashion bunny's ears by halving a banana vertically, then slicing each banana in half horizontally. Still using a knife, trim each banana piece so one end of banana is pointed. Insert on ice cream ball with toothpicks, so they will resemble ears. Serve at once.

**Denver
Dividends**

181

Maple Snow

Here is a recipe strictly for the kids to make all by themselves. As our first unblemished snow falls, tell your favorite youngster to go outdoors to fill a cup with snow. Happily, with continuing snowfalls, this simple recipe continues to excite the younger members of the family all winter long.

Remind your young cook to have all the other ingredients for this recipe ready before he brings in the clean snow. No snow? Simply place ice cubes in food processor bowl fitted with steel blade. Process. After a deafening sound, crushed ice soon miraculously appears. Once kids know how, they can safely use a food processor without too much supervision.

Paper cups are not recommended for this recipe, as they often collapse when snow or ice melts.

¼-½ cup pure maple syrup
4 cups (or mugs) filled with fresh snow or crushed ice

For 4 servings

Pour maple syrup into pan and heat until maple syrup is warm. Remove pan from heat. If your young helper is attuned to the microwave oven, pour maple syrup into a measuring cup. Place in microwave and push reheat button 20 seconds (80% power) to warm. Remove cup from microwave.

The cup or mug filled with snow or crushed ice should be mounded on the top. Drizzle one Tablespoon (or more) warm maple syrup over each snow cup or mug. Then lick to eat and enjoy it.

Pineapple Extravaganza

When you are searching for a knock-'em-dead dessert and discover Pineapple Extravaganza, search no more. The oh's and ah's from your appreciative guests, complimenting your dessert choice, more than compensate for any last minute trouble in the assembling and baking (only 6 minutes) of this elegant pineapple presentation.

Another bonus for this dessert is that any novice cook can try it without fear or trepidation. It is a dessert impossible to ruin.

4 small pineapples
Aluminum foil to cover
  fronds (leaves)
⅓ cup Kirsch cherry
  liqueur

Serves 8

Halve pineapple horizontally and do not remove fronds. With a sharp knife, cut around edges of shell to release fruit. Then cut fruit into cubes. Remember to leave shells intact. Reserve pineapple cubes.

Cover every frond completely with aluminum foil so no leaves are showing. Divide pineapple cubes evenly and replace in each shell. Sprinkle about 1 Tablespoon Kirsch on top of pineapple cubes in each shell.

FOR THE ICE CREAM LAYER:
1 qt. vanilla ice cream

Remove ice cream from freezer to refrigerator so that it becomes just soft enough to scoop. Under no circumstances allow the ice cream to soften enough to become runny, as firm ice cream is vital to this presentation.

JUST BEFORE SERVING:
8 egg whites
½ cup superfine sugar

Preheat oven to 400°.

In an electric mixer, beat egg whites just until they peak. Add sugar, one teaspoon at a time. Wait until it is incorporated into egg whites before adding the next teaspoon sugar. Continue beating until sugar is well mixed into egg whites. (Meringue can be made 15 minutes ahead.)

Just before baking, place a large scoop of vanilla ice cream on top of cut-up pineapple in each shell. Spoon meringue over entire surface of ice cream and cut-up pineapple to seal. Place pineapple shells on large flat pan(s) or broiler pan(s).

Bake 6 minutes or until meringue is golden brown. Remove aluminum foil from fronds. Serve each pineapple on a large individual plate. Serve at once.

Watermelon Balls
with Raspberry Ice

What a brilliant example of cool entertaining, using the season's bounty! Served at a committee meeting luncheon or on a buffet table for a summer party, this dessert evokes nothing but raves. Both its imaginative presentation and cooling taste make a hot summer day seem cool.

One watermelon, carefully chosen for boat shape
2 oz. Kirsch cherry liqueur
1 cup fresh mint leaves, stems removed, coarsely chopped
3 quarts raspberry ice (sherbet)
¾ cup chocolate morsels

GARNISH:
Mounds of watermelon balls
Additional mint sprigs

FOR SERVING:

TO SERVE:

Serves 12-16

Refrigerate watermelon until well chilled. Slice the top off horizontally. Cut as near surface as possible. Using a melon ball cutter, scoop out as many watermelon balls as possible. Place them in a bowl. Leave watermelon rind shell with only a little fruit. Sprinkle watermelon balls with Kirsch and mint leaves. Reserve them for garnish.

If necessary to even top of shell, trim shell with a knife. Fill cavity with raspberry ice. Decorate top with chocolate morsels (or, if you are allergic to chocolate, use plumped up dark raisins, previously soaked in rum).

Place prepared melon shell on large platter or tray, preferably white, green or a solid color. Surround with mounds of watermelon balls and additional mint sprigs.

Scoop out raspberry ice. Place on an individual plate with some watermelon balls and mint sprigs. The shell is just for decoration.

Brown Palace Macaroons

The highest star in the Brown's galaxy has to be their inimitable homemade macaroons. I have tested and re-tested Chef Dole's recipe to try to relieve you of any problems when you, too, make these in a home kitchen. I am pleased with my rendition. But I must admit that to savor the most drop-dead macaroons anywhere in the world, you'll have to dine at the Palace Arms Restaurant to taste the original Brown Palace Macaroons.

Macaroons are known for their versatility, as they are equally flavorful served at a mountain picnic or backyard barbecue or for your most formal spiffy dinner at home!

8 oz. almond paste*
4 oz. (⅔ cup) superfine
** sugar**
2 egg whites

Two cookie sheets lined
** with ungreased brown**
** paper**

*Available in 8-oz. cans or jars,
usually on gourmet shelf of your
supermarket.

Makes 25

Preheat oven to 325°.

In food processor bowl fitted with steel blade, place almond paste. Process until coarsely crumbed. Add superfine sugar. Process until very well blended. It is very important for almond paste and sugar each to have the same consistency. Remove to separate bowl.

Beat egg whites until stiff and glossy. Fold gently into almond-sugar mixture. With spoon or pastry bag, mound each macaroon on lined cookie sheet. Each macaroon should be about the size of a 50 cent piece. Bake 15 to 20 minutes, with only one cookie sheet at a time in an oven. Macaroons should be light gold in color. Remove macaroons with brown paper attached to cool. When cool, release macaroons by dampening with water the back of paper. Macaroons will peel off easily. Let them rest about 30 minutes and place in waxed paper-lined cookie tin to store. Of course, hide them at once to save them for company.

Fudge Brownie Mortarboards

Have you wished for a dessert to honor a recent graduate? Fudge Brownie Mortarboards will be the center of attraction, whether you are giving a strictly family party or, also, including several friends of the graduate.

Make your own favorite chocolate brownie recipe. Into a shallow square or rectangular pan, pour batter at least ¼″ thick. Bake brownies according to your recipe directions.

If you wish, you may frost brownies: again use your favorite recipe for chocolate frosting, but frosting is an extra flourish.

When brownies are cool, cut into 16 squares. The way you cut them is of the utmost importance. Cut to resemble mortarboards, about 1½″-2″ square.

TO ASSEMBLE MORTARBOARDS:

1 package red licorice strips
1 package large marshmallows
16 brownies, frosted if desired
1 package red hots candies

Serves 8

This is such a simple operation that any five-year-old can assist you. Cut red licorice strips 1½″ long to make 16 strips. With scissors, fringe one end of each strip. These are the tassels of the mortarboards. Halve 8 marshmallows.

Take one brownie and place it on top of one marshmallow half. Place one red hot in the center of the top of each brownie to attach fringed licorice strip for tassel. Behold: edible mortarboards.

Place brownies on a white tray, if possible, and arrange in concentric circles.

Microwave Double Chocolate Cookies

It is not realistic to call these cookies "chocolate chip" as during the microwaving, the chips disappear completely. These chocolate cookies, though, are certainly presentable.

The food processor simplifies, considerably, the making of this batter. Microwaving saves more cooking time when you are cooking smaller amounts, and so it is when baking these cookies. Furthermore, there is a hidden advantage as you and your family can't dive in and eat all of them at once.

¾ cup unbleached flour
¼ cup unsweetened cocoa
½ teaspoon baking soda
½ teaspoon salt
6 Tablespoons honey, warmed, or ½ cup granulated sugar
¼ cup brown sugar
4 oz. unsalted butter, chilled, cut up
1 egg
1 teaspoon vanilla
½ cup semi-sweet chocolate morsels (from 6-oz. package)
½ cup pecans, chopped (optional)

Makes about 50 cookies

Sift together flour, cocoa, baking soda and salt.

Into food processor bowl fitted with steel blade, pour honey or granulated sugar. Add brown sugar, chilled butter, egg and vanilla. Process to mix. Attach funnel to feed tube of food processor and pour flour mixture through funnel, as motor continues to run. Process to mix. Pour into a separate bowl. Add chocolate morsels. Add pecans, if desired. Wrap dough in plastic wrap and refrigerate at least 30 minutes.

To microwave: cover a piece of stiff cardboard (can be round or oblong to fit microwave oven) with waxed paper. With a teaspoon, drop cookies carefully on waxed paper in a circle. (Each cookie should be about ½ teaspoon dough.)

Microwave baking time (60%) will vary:

8 cookies—2½ minutes at bake
Turn cardboard; add 30 seconds.
Turn cardboard; add 20 seconds.

6 cookies—2 minutes at bake.
Turn cardboard; add 20 seconds.
Turn cardboard; add 10 seconds.

3 cookies—1 minute at bake
Look to see if an additional 10 seconds is needed.

Caution: microwaving these cookies on a paper plate covered with waxed paper, instead of cardboard, does not work!

Cool cookies at least 8 minutes before removing from waxed paper. Remember microwave cooking time continues a few minutes after cookies are removed from microwave oven.

Denver Dividends

187

Almond Bark Candy

This is the perfect economical candy to make at the very last minute. For example, you have just discovered the party you are attending tonight is to celebrate a birthday or an anniversary, and you have no appropriate present on hand to take.

There are several techniques for preparing Almond Bark, so if you haven't yet invested in a microwave, use either a double boiler or a regular oven.

A gift of this matchless but effortless candy is invariably received with deep gratitude by the lucky recipient. But remember that it is equally good served when you are either hosting a picnic or just eating at home, in any season.

Incidentally, making Almond Bark Candy at home costs you about two-fifths of what the candy store would charge.

½-⅔ cup slivered almonds
8 oz. (from a 24-oz.
package) vanilla candy
coating

Preheat regular oven to 375°.

Scatter almonds on cookie sheet. Place cookie sheet in oven. Watch until almonds turn golden, usually about 4 to 5 minutes, rather than brown. Remove from oven at once.

TO MICROWAVE:
One flat glass plate
or flat microwave dish

Place candy coating on plate or dish (a deeper dish will take longer). Microwave 3 minutes at 30% power to melt candy coating.

If it has bubbles and is still stiff, turn dish and microwave an additional minute or two at 30%. Remove from microwave and stir with plastic spoon or wooden spatula until velvety smooth with no bubbles.

WHEN USING DOUBLE
BOILER:

Place half of candy coating (4 oz.) in top of double boiler over gently boiling water. When melted, add remaining 4 oz. candy coating. Stir with plastic spoon or wooden spatula until velvety smooth.

WHEN USING REGULAR
OVEN:
One flat glass plate
or dish

Preheat oven to 325°.

Place candy coating on glass plate or dish. Place plate or dish on top rack of oven. Turn oven off. Leave dish 13 to 15 minutes. Remove from oven and stir with plastic spoon or wooden spatula to make velvety smooth. If there are any bubbles, return to oven to melt thoroughly.

Immediately stir slivered almonds into melted candy coating. Pour onto platter lined with waxed paper. Refrigerate about one hour to harden, but do not leave in refrigerator longer than one hour. Remove from refrigerator and break into small pieces to resemble bark.

Abacadabra—Almond Bark!

Divinity

This recipe for Divinity has been adjusted for Denver's altitude, but never make it on a humid day, as you will suffer an unmitigated disaster. Otherwise, Divinity is a candy to crave.

2½ cups sugar
½ cup light corn syrup
½ cup water
2 egg whites (use
  extra large eggs)
¼ teaspoon salt
1 teaspoon vanilla

Makes about 30 pieces

Divide sugar, corn syrup and water equally between two pans. Cook syrup in both pans over medium heat as you stir constantly (neat trick with two pans), until mixtures come to a boil. Reduce heat slightly and continue to cook without stirring.

Beat egg whites and salt in a large bowl until stiff, not dry.

When temperature in first pan reaches 248° (firm ball stage), slowly pour hot syrup over egg whites, beating constantly at high speed.

Cook the other half of syrup until it reaches 272° (soft crack stage). Beating constantly, pour this hotter syrup over first mixture, 1 tablespoon at a time, and beat thoroughly after each addition. An electric mixer does simplify this operation.

Continue to beat just until mixture begins to lose its gloss and a small amount of it holds a soft peak when dropped from a spoon. Be wary of overbeating as mixture tends to become grainy. Stir in vanilla. Drop Divinity by tablespoonsful onto waxed paper to cool.

Strawberry Bonbons

Although these bonbons are a posh creation at any season of the year, I particularly like to serve them when strawberries are at their prime at market or freshly picked from your own garden.

These strawberries, half-coated with white candy coating and with their green stems left on, are an exquisite presentation.

This unlikely combination of a soft, juicy strawberry with the cold fondant-like coating makes them unforgettable.

Best of all, Strawberry Bonbons are a cinch to make quickly.

32 medium-size (two 1-pt. baskets) strawberries
6 oz. (from a 24-oz. package) vanilla candy coating

Serves 8

To melt candy coating, see recipe for Almond Bark Candy, page 188. For dipping purposes, candy coating must be smooth and completely melted. Also, it must stay warm. If it should harden, heat again, using your favorite method until it is once again smooth and velvety.

Wash strawberries gently, but do not hull. Green stems add a striking touch of color. Dip strawberry in candy coating so that strawberry is only halfway covered. Place on platter or plate lined with waxed paper. Refrigerate at once to harden, but prepare Strawberry Bonbons not more than 4 hours before serving as, otherwise, they become too juicy.

For any fruit variation, use your own imagination. Long-stemmed cherries or grapes will work nicely, but avoid fruit slices that are inclined to be too juicy.

Treasured Homemade Eggnog

This heavenly concoction we traditionally serve to our guests at our annual Christmas morning open house. You can well expect every guest to ask for several refills. After all, merry making at Christmas comes just once a year.

The difference in taste between homemade eggnog and store-bought eggnog is incredible. Discover the difference for yourself. Please remember to toast this cook as you imbibe your homemade eggnog.

1 dozen eggs
1 quart bourbon
6 oz. dark rum
1 cup honey, slightly
**   warmed, or 2 cups**
**   superfine sugar**
2 quarts milk
1 pint whipping cream,
**   whipped**
Cinnamon
Nutmeg, freshly grated

One punch bowl and
**   punch cups**

For 24 punch cups

Separate eggs. In bowl of large electric mixer (or make in two batches), place egg yolks and beat until light yellow. Add bourbon and rum slowly as beating continues. Add honey or sugar and milk. Beat until well mixed. Pour into punch bowl.

Fold in whipped cream. Beat egg whites until stiff and glossy. Fold in egg whites. Sprinkle cinnamon and grate nutmeg on top of eggnog. Freshly grated nutmeg is the clincher.

Denver Dividends

The
Coffee
Bag

Chapter IX

The Coffee Bag

The habit of drinking coffee has long been and continues to be a way of life. In foreign countries, people meet and congregate at coffee houses. There they discuss business, participate in social gatherings, and even have intimate tête-à-têtes. Sharing a cup of coffee in a coffee house is far more economical than buying alcoholic drinks at a bistro. Besides, a certain camaraderie, found nowhere else, exists in coffee houses.

In the United States, everyone has his own coffee drinking pattern. For the working person, the coffee break is a necessary time to relax while visiting with fellow workers, and most importantly, to gather strength for the rest of the day's chores. For the person at home, coffee is sipped while carrying a half-filled coffee cup around the house most of the morning. A corollary to this is inviting one's neighbor to "Come on over for a cup of coffee".

If the coffee habit is yours, drinking a cup of hot perfect coffee in the morning, alone or with a friend, girds you for whatever the day may bring. With the spiraling cost of coffee, remember not to throw any coffee down the drain. Instead, pour leftover coffee into a glass or small pitcher to be safely harbored in your refrigerator, where it will be available for treats during the day. The zenith is sharing coffee with someone special or special friends after the evening meal when the cup of coffee is the final jewel in the crown of the repast. Drinking coffee together promotes relaxation as well as ambiance.

How much coffee is safe for you to drink daily? The amount, of course, depends on your individual tolerance to caffeine. Certainly, the daily drinking of one or two cups of coffee usually is of no consequence. But when one drinks seven cups, or more, of coffee daily, one overindulges. If guilty, try to cut down on the amount in order to stay healthy.

The caffeine in coffee you drink produces a temporary high-energy level and stimulates your brain temporarily, even your memory. Several over-the-counter drugs called "uppers" are primarily made with caffeine. Drinking coffee at night has contradictory effects as far as sleep is concerned. Some people will be so "turned on" and their minds will be so stimulated that sleep may be impossible. For others, drinking coffee late at night will produce just the opposite effect: an aura of well-being leading to sleep. Again, the affect of coffee on you will be individual, and may vary, depending on your physical condition.

Coffee Equipment

What equipment you buy or use to make coffee will depend on where the coffee is to be made. When backpacking in the mountains, or catching fresh trout while camping out, you will be brewing coffee over a campfire. No doubt, you will be using an antiquated coffeepot. Be sure it's clean and not rusty inside. When coffee grounds are placed in the bottom of a large outdoor coffeepot filled with water, a reliable technique for settling the coffee grounds, so they will not be poured into the coffee cups with the coffee, is to put your empty eggshells into the pot, too.

The choice of which coffee maker for your kitchen is up to you. What process of coffee making do you prefer? Do you want to percolate the coffee over a gas or electric burner on your stove? Or, will you opt for an electric coffee maker which uses paper filters for the coffee while it is brewing? Some electric coffee makers even boast clocks, which supposedly will have the coffee ready for you on the dot at a certain time in the morning. The worst drawback to an electric coffee maker is that it will keep coffee, after it is made, warm, but not hot. Making coffee is a breeze, whatever way you choose.

Whole or Ground Beans?

Decide whether you wish to buy already-ground vacuum-packed cans of coffee or fresh coffee beans. The latter course will be worth the extra cost for true coffee devotees. Using coffee beans produces a more flavorful cup of coffee with less caffeine.

If you have decided on buying coffee beans, still another decision awaits you. Do you want the beans ground at market for you, after you have purchased them? Or do you want to bring the beans back to your kitchen and grind them yourself, just before brewing the coffee? When buying coffee beans, have them packaged in one pound bags, unless you are planning to feed an army at your house.

Storing Coffee

Unopened vacuum-packed coffee in cans has a shelf life of six months, but once the can is opened, coffee will deteriorate after one week. So remember, an opened can will keep better in your refrigerator.

When you choose to buy whole or ground whole coffee beans, where do you store them? Buy them sparingly, as they retain their maximum strength only two weeks. At home, do not put these bags of coffee beans on shelves with other stored commodities. Rather, keep them either in the freezer (my choice) or, at least, in the refrigerator to use as needed.

Coffee Beans Grow on Trees

Amazingly, Louis XIV of France, a true coffee connoisseur himself, was given one five-foot coffee tree of Ethiopian origin for propagation purposes. The story goes that King Louis sent the seedlings from his small coffee tree to all the French colonies around the world, with the result that today there are billions of Arabica plants around the world, all sprouting from one royal forebear.

A coffee tree, more of a shrub than a tree, takes five years to mature. Before fruition, delicate white blossoms appear, similar to sweet-scented jasmine. After two months, coffee blossoms disappear and are replaced by green cherries. These take six months to ripen, turning first to red and then to a blackish red.

Hand-picked ripe coffee cherries are pulped to reveal two green coffee beans. When dried and hulled, they are graded for weight and size, and finally hand-inspected to remove impurities or imperfect beans. The green coffee beans are then packed in bags, weighing around 132 lbs., and transported to storehouses and eventually shipped overseas. To provide beans for one pound of roasted coffee grounds, 2,000 hand-picked coffee cherries are needed. This is slightly more than the annual crop of one average coffee tree. Think of this significant ratio the next time you moan at the price of coffee at market.

Arabica (pronounced air-a-BEE-ca) is the world's best coffee bean, accounting for three-fourths of the world's coffee market. Although Arabica beans are blended into a medley of coffee beans, roasted and eventually found in cans at markets, Arabica beans are also sold whole.

The only other important coffee bean is the Robusta. Although it has an unpleasant taste, producing a quite sour cup of coffee, the Robusta coffee tree has proven economically attractive to coffee growers because it is disease-resistant with a yield more than double that of Arabica beans.

Varieties of Beans

Many would-be coffee drinkers are befuddled when, seeking to buy whole coffee beans, they see a vast array of coffee choices. Each barrel or case full of beans has a glamorous name, usually from some country far away. Which kind to buy?

Coffee beans are sometimes identified by the country in which they were grown or sometimes by their individual roast. "Kenya" and "Columbia" coffee beans hail from Africa and South America respectively, while "French Roast" connotes a dark roast, rather than meaning that the beans originated in France.

Besides those coffee beans originating in exotic places, there are also American coffee beans, meaning ones grown in the Western Hemisphere. The most well-known are Jamaica Blue Mountain and Kona. With several coffees, the roast itself is responsible for the flavor. Dark roasts include espresso, Vienna and French roast.

Do not overlook the possibility of buying decaffeinated whole beans. If you cannot tolerate caffeine or if coffee keeps you awake at night, you will appreciate that tip.

If you are puzzled about the blending of coffee beans, here are some ideas from the experts. Try a mixture of coffee beans, half Columbia and half Kenya. Or, mix three-eighths each of Brazil and Columbia and one-fourth Kenya. My pet combination is the blend of equal parts of Java, Mocha and Columbia.

As a consumer, you have three options when buying blended coffees. Buy a standard or house blend made to a manufacturer's specifications. Or, ask the market to prepare a blend to your own formula. Finally, you can blend your coffee beans at home, if you wish. In any event, at coffee's soaring price today, handle coffee beans with care and learn all you can about which beans best suit your taste buds.

Grinding Coffee Beans

If you are just commencing to buy whole coffee beans, at the beginning it may be easier to have the store grind the beans for you. But as you become a veteran coffee maker, you will want to grind your own combinations.

If time is of no consequence to you, you might be amused by grinding your beans by hand, but, for most of us, an electric grinder is mandatory. When purchasing an electric grinder, some considerations are: appearance, cost, ease of grinding and, most important, durability. Also on your check list should be how many beans the grinder will hold (recall how many cups of coffee you will usually make), how difficult it will be to clean and the noise it will produce. Another point to consider is how you will remove the ground coffee from the grinder, and whether or not that procedure becomes a production or is easy to do.

Basics of Brewing a Good Cup of Coffee

1. Begin with clean equipment! Credit the famous German statesman, Bismarck, with the prescription: *"The recipe for making good coffee is simple: use a new pot every time."* Although a bit far-fetched, his advice is still useful. If coffee brewing equipment is not washed, or at least rinsed, after each use, it collects a visible oily film, adding a bitter taste to the coffee. A no-no is to clean a coffee maker with soap, as it leaves a residue making your coffee repugnant.

   The proper way to clean coffee equipment is to brush or wipe it out, using hot water. Then, rinse it with more hot water. If you need a stronger cleanser, try a baking soda solution but rinse thoroughly. Baking soda neutralizes existing flavors without leaving any trace of impurities. If your equipment still does not seem clean, run it through a complete brewing cycle, using one part distilled vinegar to four parts water. Follow this cycle with two additional brewing cycles using only water, to flush out any remaining traces of vinegar.
2. Use the best water available. Since Colorado glories in such good and pure water, there is no need to use distilled water. Do begin your coffee operation with cold water. Most thermostatic controls of automatic brewing systems require the use of cold water. The main reason not to use hot water is that often hot water pipes have mineral deposits which impart a flat taste to coffee.

3. Choose the correct grind of coffee for the coffeepot you are using. Never put anything but fine or vacuum grind in a vacuum coffee maker, which brews coffee in one to four minutes. Use drip grind for a drip pot which brews in four to six minutes. Of course, use regular grind in any pot which takes longer than six minutes to brew.

4. For best results in coffee making, use the full capacity of your coffee maker, and never less than three-fourths of the capacity. In fact, making just four cups of coffee is not really recommended. Estimate your brewing time properly and consistently, unless you have an automatic coffee maker which does that job for you. All the prime elements of coffee are brewed quickly in the proper time frame. After that, it is downhill: since the desirable elements are already extracted from the coffee, it becomes bitter.

   NEVER BOIL COFFEE!!! That is verboten. When coffee is boiled, an undesirable flavor change occurs. Serve coffee promptly after brewing. Reheated coffee loses its delicious taste and fragrance.

5. When making coffee, measure coffee and water accurately, rather than guess-estimating. Experts suggest using two leveled Tablespoons coffee (pull knife blade across filled tablespoon to level it) with ¾ cup (or 6 fluid oz.) water for each cup of coffee. You do not need an extra "spoonful for the pot", as the pot does not drink coffee.

6. Use instant coffee only when absolutely necessary, as it will never produce the top-notch taste and flavor of a well-brewed cup of coffee.

Coffee in Cooking

The more you cook, the more apt you are to see coffee listed as an ingredient in many recipes. Some cooks use coffee to baste meats, such as hams and lamb roasts, to impart a special mocha flavoring. Coffee is used to make ham with red-eye gravy, for example.

The other primary use of coffee in recipes is as a flavor-enhancer for baked goods - be it a mocha cake or a mocha pie or whatever. The flavor of carmelized fruits improves with a dash of strong coffee. In fact, you may use coffee in almost any dish you are concocting, but do not be over zealous and add more coffee than the recipe calls for, lest the dish you are making float away.

Coffee Dessert Drinks

In these days, when half the world is dieting and the other half is thinking about doing so, coffee dessert drinks are always popular. Coffee is not nutritious and has only five calories per cup, so a coffee dessert drink is seldom calorie-laden. My favorite recipes for Café Brûlot Diabolique and Irish Coffee are spelled out for you.

It is a very pleasant touch after dinner is finished to have coffee served in another room (or another area of the same room), away from the tired table where dinner was just completed. Although most people no longer wish cream and sugar with their coffee, you should have both available. I like to serve coffee with slices of candied ginger, as the two flavors synchronize so well.

Many people today will prefer espresso for their after-dinner coffee. The ritzy machine to make espresso is fun to use but does take up valuable storage space. Espresso can be brewed like ordinary coffee.

My recipes including coffee are a small sampling of various ways in which to use coffee in cooking. No doubt as you peruse other cookbooks and steal recipes from your family and friends, you will find innumerable ways to use this special transformer of recipes and flavors: coffee.

The Coffee Bag

Swedish Roast Lamb
with Coffee

Trust the Swedes, those clever cooks, to fantasize and utilize such a splendid way to roast a lamb. Coffee is such a wonderful marinade, particularly for lamb, that it is a wonder we do not use it more frequently.

**One 4-5 lb. trimmed
leg of lamb
Pepper, freshly ground,
to taste
1 medium-size onion,
chunked
2 carrots, chunked
1 celery stalk, without
leaves, chunked
½ cup chicken stock
½ cup very strong coffee**

**FOR THE JUS
(PAN DRIPPINGS):
1½ Tablespoons fresh dill,
stemmed, or 2 teaspoons
dried dill**

**TO SERVE:
Several sprigs of parsley**

Serves 8

Preheat oven to 400°.

Trim off any remaining fat and skin from lamb. Discard. Grind pepper over lamb and rub in, using your fingers to massage. Place lamb, topside down (where skin used to be) in roaster, preferably on a rack so it will not absorb grease. Scatter onion around lamb. Bake 30 minutes. Turn lamb upside-down. Bake an additional 15 minutes.

Remove lamb from roaster to pour off excess grease and fat from pan. Return lamb to roaster with carrots and celery around it. Reduce heat to 375°. Continue to roast lamb for 30 minutes. Pour chicken stock over lamb and continue to roast an additional 15 minutes. Pour half of coffee over lamb. Continue to roast an additional 30 minutes as you baste lamb often (about every 7 to 8 minutes), with remaining coffee. Remove lamb to warm platter. Keep warm.

Strain juices from roaster and pour into a small pan. Add dill. Skim off as much fat as possible.

When platter is to be presented at table, garnish platter by scattering sprigs of parsley around roast lamb. Carve lamb into medium-thin slices. Serve hot. Pass a sauceboat filled with the hot jus to spoon over lamb.

Anniversary Cake

Everyone knows about several-tiered wedding cakes, but what does a cook serve to celebrate his own or his friends' anniversary? This chocolate cake, with coffee as the mystery ingredient, will be the stuff of dreams long after your party is over.

Since you are saving the best for last, try to present this cake on a cake stand with a pedestal. Let the host or hostess cut it at table and dole out portions to the guests, who are yearning for a taste of such a masterpiece.

1 cup superfine sugar
  or ½ cup and 1 Tablespoon
  honey
¼ cup water
1 Tablespoon very strong
  coffee or 1 teaspoon
  instant espresso
6 oz. semi-sweet
  chocolate, cut up
1 teaspoon vanilla
6 Tablespoons unsalted
  butter, softened,
  cut up
5 egg yolks (reserve
  remaining 3 egg yolks
  for icing)
8 oz. pecans or walnuts,
  coarsely ground (use
  steel blade of food
  processor)
2 Tablespoons bread crumbs
8 egg whites
⅛ teaspoon salt

Two 9″ round cake pans,
  buttered
Additional butter for
  waxed paper
Sifted cocoa for pans

Serves 12

Preheat oven to 350°.

Prepare cake pans by buttering and lining bottoms with waxed paper. Butter waxed paper. Dust pans with sifted cocoa. Shake out excess.

Combine sugar or honey, water and coffee or espresso in a pan over medium heat. Stir continuously for 5 minutes. Add chocolate and vanilla. Stir until smooth and shiny. Remove pan from heat. Let cool 10 minutes.

Into food processor bowl fitted with steel blade, place butter around blades. With motor running, add the 5 egg yolks, one at a time, through feed tube. After each addition, process to mix. With motor running, pour slowly the cooled chocolate mixture, nuts and bread crumbs through feed tube. Process to mix. Pour mixture into a large separate bowl.

In another bowl or mixer, place 8 egg whites with a pinch of salt. Beat until stiff but not dry. With a rubber spatula, carefully fold one-third of beaten egg whites into chocolate mixture. Fold in remaining egg whites.

Divide batter in half and pour into prepared pans. Place in oven on middle rack. Bake about 30 minutes and remove pans from oven. (Center will be a little moist.) Cool in pans 30 minutes. Remove cakes from pans. Cool on racks 2 hours or more.

(continued on next page)

The
Coffee
Bag

FOR THE ICING:
Additional 6 oz. semi-sweet
   chocolate, cut up
1/3 cup water
Additional 2 Tablespoons
   very strong coffee or
   2 teaspoons instant espresso
1 cup and additional
   2 Tablespoons unsalted
   butter, softened, cut up
3 egg yolks
2/3 cup powdered sugar

GARNISH:
Additional 4 cups ground pecans
   or walnuts (use same nuts
   as used in cake)

TO ASSEMBLE:

Into pan over low heat, place chocolate, water and coffee or espresso. Stir constantly as mixture cooks until smooth. Remove pan from heat. Refrigerate until cold.

Into food processor bowl fitted with steel blade, place butter around steel blades. With motor running, add the 3 reserved egg yolks, one at a time, through feed tube. Process after each addition to mix. With motor running, through feed tube, pour cold chocolate mixture slowly into egg yolk mixture. When integrated, add powdered sugar. Process to mix.

On a cake stand or tray, place one cake. With small metal spatula, spread with icing. Place second cake on top of this. Spread with icing to cover top and sides of cake. Press nuts evenly into sides of cake. Keep cake in a cool place until ready to serve.

Coffee Pumpkin Flan

Serving Coffee Pumpkin Flan is a practical but effective way of using up a garden explosion of pumpkins. But if you have a red thumb instead of the proverbial green one, don't despair. Either buy a fresh pumpkin at market or cheat and use pumpkin from a can. Its flavor may not be comparable to the fresh taste, but face it: it makes this recipe easier to do.

Flans are inherited from Mexico and display a wonderful contrast in flavor: the almost-liquid caramel underneath the custard-like flan is a symphony. As a bonus, it can be made ahead and refrigerated.

¾ cup sugar
One 16-oz. can (2 cups) pumpkin or equivalent amount (2 cups) fresh pumpkin, cooked
1 teaspoon ginger
¾ teaspoon cinnamon
⅛ teaspoon ground cloves or allspice
1 Tablespoon molasses
1 Tablespoon melted butter
¼ cup and additional 1 Tablespoon honey, warmed
One 13-oz. can evaporated milk
1 Tablespoon instant coffee mixed in ¼ cup boiling water
4 eggs
1 Tablespoon arrowroot
⅛ teaspoon grated nutmeg

One 10″ pie pan

GARNISH:
½-¾ cup whipping cream, whipped
1 Tablespoon Kahlua coffee liqueur

Serves 10

Preheat oven to 350°.

Carmelize sugar in pan over medium-high heat. Pour syrup into pie pan. Coat sides and bottom of pan. Cool.

In food processor bowl fitted with steel blade, combine pumpkin, ginger, cinnamon, cloves, molasses and melted butter. Process to blend well. Remove to another bowl.

Place in food processor bowl, still fitted with steel blade, warmed honey, evaporated milk and dissolved coffee. Process to blend. With motor running, add eggs, one at a time, through feed tube. Process briefly to blend. Return pumpkin mixture to food processor bowl. Process until mixtures are integrated.

Remove ¼ cup of pumpkin mixture to a glass measuring cup and add arrowroot. Stir to mix well. Return to mixture in food processor bowl and process briefly, just to mix. Add freshly grated nutmeg. Pour mixture into carmelized pie pan. Place in bain-marie on middle rack in oven. Bake 1 to 1½ hours. Check after one hour. It is done when an inserted knife blade comes out clean. Serve warm or cool. Refrigerate if not serving immediately.

Should you wish to live it up, garnish flan with whipped cream, lightly mixed with Kahlua, piled on top of flan.

Denver Chocolate Pudding with Coffee

Actually, this is a famous old-time recipe that has emerged into popularity again today. No wonder, since it is such an enchanting moist pudding, perfect with a large scoop of French vanilla ice cream, or perhaps coffee ice cream, to crown it.

Denver Chocolate Pudding can be assembled speedily, and is such an easy recipe that it is almost disaster-proof. It is a version of a pudding-cake, consisting of a simple baking powder biscuit dough, laced with unsweetened chocolate. The batter is sprinkled with the sugars, cocoa, then covered with cold strong black coffee. During baking, the sugary crusty biscuit mixture rises to top off a rich coffee fudge sauce. Best of all, it is not cloyingly sweet and welcomes ice cream to top it.

FOR THE PUDDING:
¾ cup superfine sugar
1 cup unbleached flour
2 teaspoons baking powder
½ teaspoon salt
2 Tablespoons unsalted butter
1 oz. unsweetened chocolate
½ cup milk
1 teaspoon vanilla

One 9″ × 9″ pan, greased, dusted with sifted cocoa

FOR THE TOPPING:
½ cup light brown sugar
Additional ½ cup superfine sugar
4 Tablespoons cocoa, sifted
1-1¼ cups cold strong black coffee

Serves 8

Preheat oven to 350°.

In medium bowl, sift together sugar, flour, baking powder and salt. In the top of double boiler (or in microwave for about 30 seconds at 80% power), melt butter with chocolate. Add chocolate mixture to dry ingredients. Stir in milk and vanilla. Mix well. Spoon mixture into baking pan.

Combine brown sugar and superfine sugar with cocoa and sprinkle over batter. Pour coffee evenly over topping. Bake about 40 minutes. Remove from oven. Let cool.

Serve Denver Chocolate Pudding at room temperature, topped with ice cream.

Irish Coffee Pudding

Are you squeamish about drinking Irish Coffee after dinner, and do you believe that it will keep you awake into the wee hours? The judicious answer for you is this Irish Coffee Pudding. It's a dandy for St. Patrick's Day as Dubliners as well as Irishmen everywhere will agree, but don't forget to serve it on any of the other 364 days of the year.

6 eggs
½ cup honey, warmed
  or ¾ cup sugar
1½ cups strong black
  coffee (French Roast
  preferred)
2½ packages (2½ Tablespoons)
  unflavored gelatin dissolved
  in ¼ cup cold water
⅓-½ cup Irish Whiskey
1¼ cups whipping cream

One 6 cup (1½-qt.) soufflé
  dish or 8 individual pots
  de creme or
  8 demitasse cups
One small juice glass
  or small jar

FOR THE TOPPING:
Additional 1 cup
  whipping cream, whipped
2 Tablespoons walnuts,
  chopped

Serves 8

Separate eggs. In food processor bowl fitted with plastic blade, process briefly to combine egg yolks with honey or sugar. Heat coffee but do not let it boil. Add dissolved gelatin to hot coffee and make sure that it thoroughly melts. Add coffee mixture to food processor bowl. Process briefly.

Pour mixture into top of double boiler with water boiling in bottom pan. Whisk until coffee mixture begins to thicken. Add whiskey. Continue to whisk until mixture is thick and creamy. Remove pan from heat and refrigerate.

Beat whipping cream until stiff. Beat egg whites until firm and glossy.

When coffee mixture is on the verge of setting, fold in whipped cream. Gently fold in beaten egg whites. Pour mixture into soufflé dish. Using a flavorless vegetable oil, oil outside of small juice glass or jar. Make a well in center of Irish Coffee Pudding in soufflé dish, and put oiled glass or jar in it. Refrigerate.

Remove glass or jar from center of pudding and fill this center cavity with additional whipped cream. Just before serving, scatter chopped walnuts on top of Irish Coffee Pudding.

Café Brûlot Diabolique
(Flaming Devilish Coffee)

It was John Ringling of circus fame who queried *"What could be more sublime than to taste the delights of heaven while beholding the terrors of hell?"* His colorful gastronomic figure of speech describes the presentation of Café Brûlot Diabolique. It is guaranteed to dazzle all your guests when you serve it after dinner, preferably before a blazing fire.

Dim the lights of the room before you ignite the brandy. Slowly pour brandy from ladle into the bowl, creating a flaming cascade. A pyrotechnical display reminiscent of Molly Brown's recipe for Baked Alaska Flambé in bygone days. Another peg in the full circle of culinary extravagances.

¾ cup brandy
One or two 1″ cinnamon
  sticks
2 whole cloves
Zest of lemon, cut
  into thin strips
¼ teaspoon grated nutmeg
Zest of one orange,
  preferably removed in one
  long continuous spiral
3 sugar cubes
3½-4 cups hot strong coffee
  (could be espresso)

Serves 8

In small separate pan over medium-low heat, heat brandy.

In chafing dish, handsome heat-proof bowl or pan, over direct heat, combine all other ingredients except coffee. Heat seasonings about ten minutes until very hot throughout.

Using a heated ladle, pour in some brandy and ignite. Ladle flaming brandy into chafing dish or serving dish. While brandy is flaming, pour in hot coffee. Serve in demitasse cups.

Frosted Coffee

Frosted Coffee, made in two minutes flat, is one of my more difficult recipes. Use either your food processor or blender. Also, making Frosted Coffee is a clever way to use leftover coffee, if you are feeling guilty about throwing it away.

⅜ cup iced coffee
⅜ cup vanilla ice cream,
  barely soft
¼ cup half-and-half
  or milk

For one serving

Place all ingredients into food processor or blender. Process or whiz very briefly to blend thoroughly. Do not overprocess or overblend, as it is so sensuous to have a few ice cream lumps to punctuate the smoothness of this dessert-drink. Remember to serve it at once.

Heavenlies

Although Heavenlies were born in Palm Beach, Denver cooks, too, will succumb. You can make Heavenlies with your food processor or blender quicker than you can say *"When I go to Heaven, I hope the path along the way will be strewn with Heavenlies"*.

Once you get the hang of this recipe, experiment to find other favorite combinations of ice cream flavors and various liqueurs.

2 quarts coffee ice cream
¼ cup brandy

Serves 8

Place cartons of ice cream in refrigerator about one hour ahead to slightly soften. In food processor bowl fitted with plastic blade, place 1 quart ice cream and pour in ⅛ cup brandy. Process briefly with on-off pulse three times about 3 seconds each. The texture should be akin to a milk shake's - lumpy and gooey. Be sure that the plastic blade fits very tightly into food processor bowl so that liquid will not overflow. Immediately, pour a Heavenly into each stemmed sherbet glass.

Repeat process to make second batch of Heavenlies. If using blender, follow same directions and, also, make in two batches. Try to serve at once, very cold, before it melts.

If not serving at once, keep in deep freeze in a bowl until 10 to 15 minutes before serving time. It may be necessary to whiz ever so briefly before serving. Under no circumstances, serve in individual small bowls, as a Heavenly will become soupy, not heavenly.

Irish Coffee as the Natives Do It

Practically all recipes for Irish Coffee are misleading. In assembling Irish Coffee, there is a tricky part. This hint is seldom found in any recipe reprinted in the U.S.A.. Hold a teaspoon curved side up **across** the glass. Do not attempt to stir cream into coffee. The cream should float on top and the hot whiskey-laced coffee is then drunk through that cold cream. Sexy!

That's the way the Irish do it! My family and I were residents there one whole joyous summer. In Ireland, drinking Irish Coffee this way is a nightly ritual (following dinner) that Denverites can easily copy. Especially if you have some Irish in you.

1 heaping teaspoon sugar
1 cup strong, hot black
  coffee (French Roast
  preferable)
1 double jigger Irish
  Whiskey
1 Tablespoon double cream
  (whipping cream in U.S.A.)

One stemmed whiskey glass
  or stemmed Irish
  Coffee cup

Serves one

Warm glass or cup. Neither has to have that four-leaf clover on it, but Irish Coffee does show off better in a glass or cup with a stem.

Combine sugar and hot coffee to dissolve sugar. Stir well. Pour in the Irish Whiskey up to an inch below the rim of the glass or cup. Then pour in cream as described above.

Mocha Punch

Serving a punch is an old-time, but sometimes forgotten, custom that we should initiate again. Mocha Punch is one to cherish.

3 cups freshly made
  coffee, chilled
3 cups (1½-pts.)
  chocolate ice cream
2 Tablespoons rum or
  ½ teaspoon almond extract
⅛ teaspoon salt
1 cup whipping cream,
  whipped (reserve ½ cup
  whipped cream)

GARNISH:
Reserved ½ cup whipped cream
Freshly grated whole nutmeg
  or 1 oz. sweet chocolate

One large chilled punch
  bowl

TO SERVE:

Serves 8

Pour chilled coffee into punch bowl. Add half of the ice cream. Beat until ice cream is softened. Add rum or almond extract and salt. Fold in remainder of ice cream. Fold in whipped cream.

From punch bowl, ladle Mocha Punch into individual tall glasses. Garnish with reserved whipped cream. Grate nutmeg or sweet chocolate over top of whipped cream.

Denver
Hospitable

Chapter X

What Every House Guest Should Know
or
Advice Mother Gave But I May Have Forgotten

In today's usual do-it-yourself households, entertaining house guests ups considerably the host-hostess load. So that everyone will not be in a flap and the visit—whether for a quick overnight or for a year—will be as smooth as possible, here are some guide lines:

1. The courteous house guest always alerts his host of the date of the visit as soon as the plans are scheduled. The day of the drop-in house guest is taboo. Simultaneously, the guest-to-be advises how he will arrive and if he is expecting to eat any meal on arrival, especially dinner. He should stick to his original plan except for an emergency.

2. The wise house guest will also advise his host about departure plans along with arrival plans. If this does not occur, to stop the guessing game, the wise host should ask the house guest soon after his arrival what his specific departure plans are.

3. Once the guest is ensconced in the house of his host, house rules — not guest rules — abide. Also, the host's social plans for his guest's visit supercede guest's ideas. If the guest prefers to make his own plans instead of following the host's, the guest should stay at a hotel.

4. House guests should give an almighty try to keeping the household where he is visiting as normal as possible. House guests should adapt to the household — be it unruly children, pets or what-have-you — not the other way around.

5. Togetherness is great but the host cannot shed his daily responsibilities. Although the house guest may want to rehash shared experiences until wee morning hours, remember the host has to rise and shine even though the guest can sleep in.

6. The smart house guest does not follow his host around. The guest may be on vacation but the host is not. He still needs time alone as does the guest. The guest should go to his room, shut the door and, if he does not need shut-eye, read and keep quiet for at least two hours every day.

7. An invariable no-no: the guest should never charge any long-distance calls to the host's telephone bill. If the guest does not boast a telephone charge-card, he should ask the operator the charges or guess-estimate the amount. This money should be left with the host when the guest leaves.

8. Happier house guest households are ones where meal times are established. It is up to the house guest to be dressed and on time.

9. Should the house guest want to sleep in the morning, he should inquire if he may fix his own breakfast. The host-hostess cannot be expected to be on call to cook. The guest should never use anything from the host's refrigerator without checking. For instance, the guest may be consuming bananas that were to be an integral part of tonight's dessert, and they may be the last bananas in the whole city.

10. No guest should sit on his duff and expect to be waited on. Every guest should make his own bed and always keep his room and bath tidy. Remember the room is on loan. The guest should ask what he can do to help in the household chores. Don't expect your host to provide a car for you to drive. Nothing is more traumatic than for a host to find his car, needed for a vital errand, borrowed by his house guest on his errand.

    While laundering bed linens, towels and washcloths is the responsibility of the host/hostess, personal laundry and ironing of the guest's clothes are the guest's responsibility.

11. Not everyone can afford to bring a present when he comes—a custom with almost every foreigner—or send one later. But everyone can afford to write a prompt bread-and-butter letter. This is not much to ask in return for the free room, board and services your host has provided you. If there is a cleaning lady who has readied the guest's bedroom and will clean up after the guest, a thoughtful gesture is to leave her a small tip. If the household is a spiffy one where some outside help is employed, the house guest displays awful manners by ordering help around. This is not his prerogative. Every guest should gently give his requests to the host, never to a person the guest does not pay.

12. Throughout the guest's visit, he should retain a lively sense of humor as should his host-hostess. Smile a lot. Be cheerful, especially in the morning, and have a delightful visit together!

REMEMBER: CHILDREN AND RELATIVES WHO HAVE INDEPENDENT HOMES BECOME HOUSE GUESTS WHEN VISITING.

HAVE A LOVE-LY VISIT!

Acknowledgements

THE DEVILS
who made me do it!

Carl Sontheimer, the Cuisinart Guru, who bedeviled me into writing a Denver cookbook.

The late **Bob Lotito,** my esteemed Business Manager, who held my hand during all the rigors of writing and marketing a book, and whom I continue to miss greatly.

THE ANGELS
who helped me put it all together:

All my friends at King Soopers, especially **President Jim Baldwin** and **Gene Milne.** Gene and his fantastic staff dreamed up the layout for the book. Gene, always genial, always goes the extra mile and is very special to this book and its author.

Judy Disner, the artist, who imaginatively translated my words and recipes into fun, contemporary graphics.

Ada Friedman, proofreader extraordinaire, whose eagle eye considerably spruced up my copy. Not only does she have an enviable command of the English language, but also, she is conversant with cooks' materials and directions.

Carol Truax, who has 24 cookbooks of her own (can you believe: working on her 25th?), was a wise and trusted adviser. She can sight errors in a cookbook more than anyone I know. Carol understands why recipes will or won't work.

Elizabeth Farrar Wector, born in Denver but transplanted to San Francisco, aided in innumerable ways, as authoring and publishing are second nature to her. She also is a terrific cook, whose advice and encouragement I respect.

Jane McCotter, who emerged as my Denver volunteer editor. Not since my college days, has anyone so skillfully tightened up my prose, rerouting my sentences, but always maintaining my thought pattern. This is a far better book because of Jane's fine touch.

Phil Sheridan for his superb copyright know-how, and **Ellen Winner** for her painstaking legal expertise, and to both for their continuing enthusiastic encouragement.

Ed Pierson, whose expertise and diplomacy concerning an author's contract becomes very meaningful.

212

Bosom friends like **Rosemary Van Vleet, Pat Livingston, Nancy Petry** and **Mother** who painstakingly read the copy of various chapters and leveled with me about their feelings and findings.

New friends like newly-married **Sharon** and **Neil Bush** who read copy aloud to me until they were hoarse.

My Cousin, John Mackenzie, for continued inspiration and stimulus as he bombards me with innovative ideas about food.

Cathy Baumgartner, my indefatigable secretary, for her unswerving loyalty.

Elizabeth Peck, my girl Friday throughout the writing of the entire book, who pinch-hit from grocery shopping, to research assistant, to trying and advising on perfecting the recipes.

Stan Peckham and **Phil Thayer,** my devilish scouts, who discovered **Barbara Mussil,** my newest angel, who welcomed and warmly embraced *Denver Delicious.*

Bouquets of Basil, *the king of herbs, to:*

The ladies of the National Jewish Hospital and Asthma Center Auxiliary, who were *Denver Delicious*'s first lifeline to the Denver community.

Caroline Bancroft for permission to use material with recipes from her book, co-authored by the late May Wills, *The Unsinkable Molly Brown Cookbook.*

Clara Mitchell Humphreys, daughter, and John Clark Mitchell, grandson of Clara Mitchell, for permission to use material with recipes from *The Way To A Man's Heart* by the late Clara Mitchell.

Bouquets of Chervil, *a flavor catalyst which adds to the flavor of* Denver Delicious:

Glynn Christian (Jerusalem Artichoke Soup with Italian Sauce)

Craig Claiborne (recipe adapted from Craig Claiborne's Pancake from *The New York Times*)

Barbara Conwell, the cook's teacher

Jaynn Emery (Bronco Outasight Cake)

Richard Grausman (Rick's Grand Marnier Chocolate Soufflé)

Allan Hickerson (Beaten Biscuits)

Velma Hinton (Velma's Barbecued Spareribs)

Calvin Kunz (Cal's Sukiyaki)

Muriel Magarrell (Snow Squares with Butter Sauce)

Karl Mehlman (Brown Palace Macaroons)

Dick Olson (Dick's French Toast)

Lenore Stoddart (for her mother's recipe for Shrimp and Rice)

Marika Hanbury Tenison (recipe adapted from hers for Cornish Pasties)

Rosemary Van Vleet (Rosemary's Spoon Bread)

Index

215

217

221

JOHNSON BOOKS
1880 South 57th Court
Boulder, Colorado 80301

Please send me ____ copies of *Denver Delicious* at $9.95 per copy plus $1.00 for postage and handling. (Colorado residents add sales tax. U.S. funds only.)

Enclosed is my check or money order in the amount of $____.

Name _____

Address _____

City _____ State _____ Zip _____

FROM: Johnson Books
1880 South 57th Court
Boulder, Colorado 80301

TO:

Name _____

Address _____

City _____

State _____ Zip _____

MAILING LABEL—PLEASE PRINT

JOHNSON BOOKS
1880 South 57th Court
Boulder, Colorado 80301

Please send me ____ copies of *Denver Delicious* at $9.95 per copy plus $1.00 for postage and handling. (Colorado residents add sales tax. U.S. funds only.)

Enclosed is my check or money order in the amount of $____.

Name _____

Address _____

City _____ State _____ Zip _____

FROM: Johnson Books
1880 South 57th Court
Boulder, Colorado 80301

TO:

Name _____

Address _____

City _____

State _____ Zip _____

MAILING LABEL—PLEASE PRINT

JOHNSON BOOKS
1880 South 57th Court
Boulder, Colorado 80301

Please send me ____ copies of *Denver Delicious* at $9.95 per copy plus $1.00 for postage and handling. (Colorado residents add sales tax. U.S. funds only.)

Enclosed is my check or money order in the amount of $____.

Name _____

Address _____

City _____ State _____ Zip _____

FROM: Johnson Books
1880 South 57th Court
Boulder, Colorado 80301

TO:

Name _____

Address _____

City _____

State _____ Zip _____

MAILING LABEL—PLEASE PRINT